COMPOSERS

Francis Poulenc

by Benjamin Ivry

Phaidon Press Limited
Regent's Wharf
All Saints Street
London N1 9PA

First published 1996

ISBN 0 7148 3503 X

A CIP catalogue record for this book is available from the British Library

Printed in Singapore

Frontispiece, a skilled pianist as well as multi-talented composer, Poulenc entertained his friends in private soirées, and the general public in recordings and concerts.

Contents

Preface

France is famous among researchers worldwide for its user-unfriendly libraries: although more frequently open than libraries elsewhere in the Mediterranean, French research centres are sometimes crippled by librarians who look at researchers rather as a bullfighter looks at the bull. This may be why some of the best Poulenc research has been done in Britain (Winifred Radford and Sidney Buckland) and the USA (Carl B. Schmidt), where more humanist libraries exist than in the composer's home country. The notable recent exception in France, Myriam Chimènes, benefited in preparing her monumental collection of Poulenc's correspondence from the protective armour of the research assocation, the CNRS. Despite the drawbacks of some French institutions, the human contacts can be charming. I would like to thank Sidney Buckland, Myriam Chimènes and Renaud Machart for their kind help and patience in clarifying some points. Myriam Chimènes's book of letters, like Sidney Buckland's somewhat shorter version in English, adds a work to French literature and is an essential source for understanding the composer, giving a more complete portrait than even his intimate friends could convey. Among those who knew Poulenc, Madeleine Milhaud, Jeannine Worms, Robert Shaw, Gabriel Tacchino, Allen Hughes and Hugues Cuénod had the most consistently amusing and enlightening things to say about him.

For matters discographical, I have benefited over the years from some of America's most erudite record connoisseurs, like Karl Schrom and Richard Warren, both of New Haven, Connecticut. For his sage philosophy about writing books on musical subjects, I thank the multi-talented Patrick O'Connor. About French culture I have learned much from two American authorities who had the wisdom to stay out of France in order to be inspired by its culture: Richard Howard and the late (much regretted) James Ingram Merrill. Other American friends who have provided considerable practical help, encouragement and delight include James H. Marrow and Emily Rose, Harold and Carol Rolfe, Carolyn Kizer and John Woodbridge. For hospitality and encouragement in France at various stages of the project I am most grateful to the following, who showed me that Paris is not completely deprived of the sort of joy that Poulenc experienced: Simone Boué, Yannick Guillou, Eloisa Helena, Marcelo Ferreira, Yndi Ferreira, Florian Cadier and Rogério de Souza Poly.

For particular encouragement at a difficult time, thanks are gratefully offered to Muriel Spark and Penelope Jardine, and to the late E. M. Cioran, an insightful and endearing guide to the arts in France since the 1930s and a friend sorely missed. Finally, my thanks to the staff at Phaidon Press, especially the editors Norman Lebrecht, Peter Owens, Roger Sears and Ingalo Thomson, picture researcher Polly Clayden and Hans Dieter Reichert of hdr design.

Benjamin Ivry
Paris, 1996

Introduction

Francis Poulenc (1899–1963) is one of the most popular composers of his century. In Britain and the USA he is seen as a very Parisian composer, revealed in humorous, insouciant works like the ballet *Les Biches* and the opera *Les Mamelles de Tirésias*; in France he is admired for his fine chansons and religious music, culminating in the magnificent opera, *Dialogues des Carmélites*. Yet neither insouciant humorist nor ardent religious spirit categorize the man. He was often manically comic, but suffered also from lengthy depressive cycles. One critic, Claude Rostand, summed him up as 'half bad boy, half monk', but this formula is just a little too glib.

Until recently, it was hard to make any judgements about Poulenc at all: his letters, essential for interpreting his life and works, had only been published in expurgated form. The British scholar and translator Sidney Buckland was the first, in 1991, to offer a generous selection of the composer's letters; her work was completed in French by the researcher Myriam Chimènes in a publication over one thousand pages long. These letters have opened new vistas in understanding the chronology and intent of Poulenc's works. In addition, in 1993 French critic Renaud Machart published another unexpurgated text, Poulenc's *Journal de mes mélodies*, which had appeared previously, but with one third of its contents missing. This new material suggests that past generalizations in Poulenc's life, such as the monk and bad boy comparisons, were caricatures of the reality. Only in 1995 did a full catalogue of Poulenc's work appear, compiled by the American musicologist Carl B. Schmidt.

In 1937, Poulenc told a friend that he hoped he might be 'an almost great composer'. This qualification of the adjective may be justified, but the composer managed nevertheless to create some entirely admirable works. His music is melodic, lyrical, and emotionally expressive, in a clearly tonal framework. His works flow gracefully, the epitome of French lightness. Already these qualities distanced him from much of the current of modern classical music. Instead of producing arcana for a minority public, Poulenc wrote showpieces: communication to an audience was a key to his art.

To posterity, Poulenc is certainly one of the major composers of his generation. Although he was much influenced by Igor Stravinsky's neo-classical style, he was not an innovator like his friends and contemporaries Darius Milhaud and Arthur Honegger, who both experimented with new harmonies and rhythms. Poulenc displayed an almost exasperating versatility, with a range of musical expression – from the rollicking hilarity of the *Babar* suite to the moving song 'C' – that outshone his contemporaries. He was not concerned with music of the future, he just wanted to please an audience and himself. Poulenc looked for influence to Erik Satie, yet he pillaged older masters – from Mozart to Saint-Saëns – for musical ideas; and it is this anthological aspect of Poulenc's music that makes it particularly hard to pin him to a specific musical identity. Most general histories have offered little other information than identifying him as a member of the group Les Six (the quintessentially Parisian group of young composers in the early 1920s, linked more by friendship than by common musical style). He has been accused, not without reason, of having a problem with attention span; yet he took great pains over the formal structure of his works. The label of 'charming, minor master' has been often applied to him.

One reason behind the underestimation of Poulenc during much of his lifetime was his open homosexuality at a time when only the most prestigious cultural figures, such as Jean Cocteau, could get away with such frankness. Poulenc's letters, not only good reading but a revealing biographical analysis of his own works, make it clear that his sexuality was central to his composition, in so far as several of his major works – including the sacred – were inspired by his lovers. His life and art set an example of a deeply troubled artist who managed to master his inner anguish and create a significant œuvre.

But if for no other reason than the fact that he is the most French of composers in the generation after Ravel, Poulenc merits respect and serious study.

I

Childhood and Youth 1899–1919

At twenty, Poulenc had already decided to be a musician, but his emotional life was far from settled: sexual identity confusion and matters of the heart would be addressed during his twenties.

What you sometimes refer to as my 'bad boy' side developed quite naturally at Nogent-sur-Marne … That was my idea of paradise.

Francis Poulenc,
Entretiens avec Claude Rostand

Childhood and Youth 1899–1919

Francis Poulenc was born on 7 January 1899, at 2 place des Saussaies in Paris's frigidly wealthy eighth arrondissement. The family could afford to live near the Presidential palace, the Elysées, because Poulenc's father was one of the founders of the company that became the chemicals giant, Rhône-Poulenc. Today, the wealth of that company makes Parisians' eyes glint. Poulenc always lived very comfortably, but during his lifetime the fortune involved with Rhône-Poulenc was not quite the Arabian Nights' hoard it later became. The composer had to work in order to maintain his lifestyle.

Poulenc's father Émile (1855–1917), originally from Aveyron in the Midi-Pyrénées region, was a provincial man and a pious Catholic who liked music by Beethoven and César Franck. His mother Jenny (1865–1915) was from a family of Paris craftsmen in tapestry, bronze, and carpentry. With a Parisian's turn-of-the-century gaiety, she added the lightness which became an essential part of Francis's personality; she preferred Mozart, Chopin, and 'adorable bad music'. From his father, as well as an inclination towards church-going, Poulenc inherited the rough-featured ugliness of a French *paysan.* His mother, more refined in looks, gave him a capital gift: the love of music. Years later he would dedicate his opera *Dialogues des Carmélites* to 'the memory of my mother, who revealed music to me; to Claude Debussy, who gave me the taste for writing it; to Monteverdi, Giuseppe Verdi, Modest Mussorgsky ...' By linking his mother to the names of composers, Poulenc clearly viewed her as an admirable musician in her own right.

His mother's brother, Marcel Royer (1862–1945), was known as Uncle Papoum, after Francis's initial attempts to pronounce the word *parrain* (godfather). Papoum was a frenetic theatre buff and opera fan, who loved to tell tales of his youth as an art student, when he socialized with Toulouse-Lautrec. As with the poet W. H. Auden and his 'Uncle Henry', a young homosexual creative artist can learn a lot from a wealthy bachelor uncle who is mad about the arts.

At the age of two, Francis was given a white toy piano with cherries painted on it, and pretended to 'sight-read' on this piano everything from department store catalogues to railway timetables. When he was five, more formal piano lessons began with his mother and by the age of eight he was studying piano with a certain Mademoiselle Melon, assistant of a noted teacher, Cécile Boutet de Montvel, herself the niece of César Franck. It was around the age of eight that he discovered the music of Debussy, although he could not as yet play it. He was however able to play and sing Schubert's song cycle *Die Winterreise,* in French translation, and dreamed of becoming a tenor after his Uncle Papoum introduced him to a friend, the famed tenor Edmond Clément (1867–1928). But Francis's voice changed at fourteen, 'leaving me with a pitiful composer's voice'.

Never an earth-shaking beauty, the adolescent Poulenc was likened by one friend to a 'young elephant'. Although his looks did not improve, ugliness never hampered a voracious gay sex life.

Poulenc hastened to leave the chilly confines of Paris's snobby eighth arrondissement, where the upper-class life bored him to tears.

– Rue de Vienne. – Rue de Rome.
EST

Igor Stravinsky in his prime, in a photo from 1925: Poulenc worshipped the Russian for his 'gigantic muscles'.

In 1914 he went to the Casino de Paris to hear Pierre Monteux conduct Igor Stravinsky's *Le Sacre du Printemps* ('The Rite of Spring'), and became a fan of Stravinsky for life. The première of the ballet the previous year was danced to the choreography of Nijinsky, and provoked one of the artistic scandals of the twentieth century. The seeming 'paganism' of the music shocked the refined ballet milieu. Those who came to hear the score performed as orchestral work alone, as Poulenc did, had more admiration for *Le Sacre*, and without the dancers as visual distraction, the superb conducting talents of Pierre Monteux were in the forefront.

Poulenc's traditionalist father told Francis, 'Poor boy, you do have odd taste in music!' A culturally sophisticated fifteen year old, Francis kept scores to new music like Stravinsky's *Petrushka* and *Le Sacre*, Bartók's *Allegro barbaro*, and Schoenberg's Six Little Pieces on his piano stand, and he knew all of Debussy's and Ravel's works. His lifelong love affair with the gramophone began early as well: as a boy he would go to the Maison Pathé on the boulevard des Italiens, where listeners placed tokens in slots to hear records. During one of these visits, in 1914, Poulenc noticed that a favourite French pianist of his, Edouard Risler, had produced a new recording. Risler was playing the *Idylle* from the *Pièces pittoresques* by a composer Poulenc at that time regarded as minor – Emmanuel Chabrier (1841–94). From the moment that Poulenc put a token in the slot of the automatic listener, his life changed. Decades later he was to recall in his book *Emmanuel Chabrier*, 'Even today I tremble with emotion in thinking of the miracle that was produced: a harmonic universe suddenly opened in front of me, and my music has never forgotten this first loving kiss.'

Chabrier's tender and subtle *Idylle* does indeed create a universe; it has a trembling, shimmering, and pliant atmosphere, offering a view through the trees of an eighteenth-century landscape. To Poulenc, a musical young man devoted to beauty, *Idylle* gave a glimpse of the finest things that life and art could offer. Poulenc would ever after think of paintings in terms of his own music; they helped him to create a 'landscape' in each work. Chabrier, himself an art collector, subscribed to this artistic credo as well.

Francis was familiar with modern literature before he was ten, thanks to a young friend, Raymonde Linossier, who was to play a most important role in his life. He had met her when their families were taking a cure at Vichy, and together they recited by heart abstruse poems by Mallarmé. Raymonde took Francis to Adrienne Monnier's bookstore Aux Amis des Livres on the rue de l'Odéon in Paris's sixth arrondissement. There he heard famous writers read their works: Paul Valéry, André Gide, Paul Claudel, Valéry Larbaud, Guillaume Apollinaire, Léon-Paul Fargue, and others. Some of these writers, like Valéry and Claudel, were poor readers of their own works, and Poulenc may have learned, by negative example, of the importance of the presentation in sound of great texts. In Poulenc's song settings the voice of the writer would always remain important to him.

His childhood was not wholly spent reading and playing music; he holidayed at his grandparents' country home at Nogent-sur-Marne, a few kilometres east of Paris. Until he was twenty-five, Poulenc regularly visited the Nogent riverside, and there he adored the boats, the dances to accordion music (*bals musettes*), *frites* and cheap wine; he also heard popular music by *chansonniers* like Vincent Scotto and Henri-Marius Christiné. Far removed from the bandying-about of aesthetic judgements in Monnier's bookstore, at Nogent a visitor could let down his guard and relax, uncritically enjoying sensual pleasures. It was a kind of paradise for Francis, for whom comfy, nice fun was always a priority (his parents paid a nanny to look after him until he was fifteen, when Nanny was reluctantly let go). The Nogent experience may have been decisive in Poulenc's later choice of lovers among working-class, non-intellectual men.

Poulenc's mentor, the pianist Ricardo Viñes, introduced young Francis into Parisian high society, a move which proved invaluable.

In 1915 Francis met one of his mentors, Ricardo Viñes (1875–1943): this great Spanish pianist, who made unsurpassed records of twentieth-century piano music, was a friend of Debussy and Ravel. He gave first performances of their works, and also those of Enrique Granados, Isaac Albéniz, and Manuel de Falla. His playing, with a heavy use of pedal, had a singular relaxation and dynamism of touch, resulting in unmatched delicacy. To Poulenc, who said of Viñes, 'I owe him everything,' he was more than a piano teacher. Poulenc learned from him some of the basic effects of the piano, such as pedalling, and said that in the performance of his own piano compositions, it was impossible to use too much pedal.

Georges Auric (1899–1983) drawn in 1921 by Jean Cocteau. Auric was a tolerant and clear-seeing counsellor to Poulenc, and one of his closest lifelong friends.

Viñes introduced Poulenc to two influential friends: a contemporary, Georges Auric, and the controversial composer Erik Satie; both served as aesthetic models for Poulenc's early years. Satie's strangeness was an example of creative courage, of not fearing to be totally bizarre – thus he was true to his artistic goals. When Poulenc met Satie in 1917, Satie's ballet *Parade* had recently been given its première with Serge Diaghilev's Ballets Russes, and Poulenc captivated the older composer with his ardent enthusiasm for the work. Satie, constantly poverty-stricken, was at first suspicious of Poulenc's wealth, but he was won over by flattery. Georges Auric was the same age as Poulenc, and already established as a musical and literary prodigy. A recognized composer at fourteen, he associated with writers like Léon Bloy, Jacques Maritain, and Apollinaire. Poulenc would solicit Auric's advice, and take his opinion seriously, for much of his early musical career.

Throughout his life, Poulenc would seek advisers to bolster and challenge his ego, liking friends of his own age to fill the role of censorious parents. Auric, like Raymonde Linossier, was a ruthless critic of Poulenc's music and of his behaviour. Later, Poulenc would benefit from the advice of the baritone Pierre Bernac and the pianist Jacques Février, who told him candidly what they thought of works in

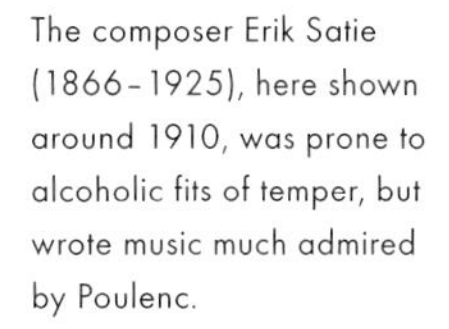

The composer Erik Satie (1866–1925), here shown around 1910, was prone to alcoholic fits of temper, but wrote music much admired by Poulenc.

Satie's ballet *Parade* was first performed on 18 May 1917 by Diaghilev's Ballets Russes, choreographed by Léonide Massine, with sets and costumes by Pablo Picasso. This production would serve as a daunting model for Poulenc's own first ballet for Diaghilev, *Les Biches*.

progress. Sometimes Poulenc reacted by destroying what he was working on, but most often he reached a salutary balance between creative *élan* and self-criticism. Poulenc made composing a social activity and would solicit opinions as early as possible in the creative process. He wrote his works alone, but no sooner were they set to paper than he liked to have some response from those whose views he respected – first among them Auric.

World War I was raging around them, and some of Poulenc's generation reacted by 'damaging themselves' in pleasure. While waiting to be called up for the carnage, wild carousing at parties was considered the only reasonable way to pass the time. Poulenc continued his piano studies, even though he was destined to enter the army before long. In 1917 he attended the première of a play by Guillaume Apollinaire, *Les Mamelles de Tirésias,* which would later be the source of one of his best works. Also that year, Poulenc was taken by Viñes to meet a well-known soprano, Jane Bathori, who gave the premières of works by Debussy, Ravel, and Satie. In Bathori's salon, he met famous older musicians, as well as Arthur Honegger, Louis Durey, and Germaine Tailleferre.

Poulenc's appetite for contacting famous musicians was revealed in a youthful prank as autograph-hunter in 1915. He wrote to composers (Debussy, Saint-Saëns, Satie, Stravinsky and Albert Roussel among them) to ask their opinion of César Franck. The fifteen-year-old Poulenc could not have cared less what they thought of Franck; he just wanted their autographs. Later, Poulenc would describe this stunt as having occurred when he was eighteen, perhaps as a reflection of his prolonged adolescence. The masters responded cordially to the unknown young man, with the best answer coming from Satie, who spoofed the spoof by answering, 'Franck's work is astonishingly Franckist, in the best sense of the term.'

Poulenc also wrote to a young composer he had recently met while playing tennis in the country – Darius Milhaud. The tubby, swarthy Milhaud, a Jew from Provence, was kind and encouraging to the youngster. To Milhaud, Francis made an outright request for an autograph, with no nonsense about César Franck.

In 1917 Poulenc's father died, two years after the death of his wife. The boy went to live with his elder sister Jeanne and her husband on the rue de Monceau, a chilly corner of Paris's eighth arrondissement. He was free and financially independent, and perhaps not coincidentally, he began to compose in earnest for the first time. His first efforts were of no lasting interest: a 1917 piano work, *Processional for the Cremation of a Mandarin*, was watered-down Stravinsky. *Rapsodie nègre*, written the same year for baritone voice, piano, string quartet, flute and clarinet, was a more original work, setting nonsense syllables supposedly written by a black poet from Liberia. Its vocal line is unexpectedly placid, given the rudeness of the 'African' words being sung, and lies above pleasing dissonances from the instrumental ensemble.

That September, Poulenc visited the Paris Conservatoire armed with an introduction to the distinguished teacher of composition Paul Vidal. In a letter to Viñes Poulenc related what happened:

I passed him the manuscript of my Rapsodie nègre. *[Vidal] read it attentively, furrowed his brow, rolled furious eyes on seeing the dedication to Erik Satie, stood up, and screamed precisely this at me: 'Your work stinks, it's inept, infamous balls ... Ah! I see you're a follower of the Stravinsky and Satie gang. Well, goodbye!', almost throwing me out the door.*

When he heard about Vidal's rejection, Satie advised, 'Laugh about it, old boy!' Undaunted, Poulenc prepared the première of *Rapsodie nègre* at the Théâtre du Vieux-Colombier in December 1917, at a concert organized by Jane Bathori. At the last minute, the scheduled baritone lost his nerve, so Poulenc took his place as vocal soloist. The work's 'charming naïveté' was praised and Poulenc won influential admirers. According to one account Maurice Ravel was present, and said, 'What's good about Poulenc is that he invents his own folklore.' The ballet impresario Serge Diaghilev was intrigued to hear that the composer was no more than an adolescent. Igor Stravinsky, who had heard from Ricardo Viñes that Poulenc had been banned from the Conservatoire by a reactionary professor who grouped his work with that of Satie and his own, arranged to have *Rapsodie nègre* printed by his London publisher, Chester Music.

Poulenc soon produced other works: the Sonata for two clarinets (1918) was a tentative attempt at a traditional three-movement sonata form, in this case Presto–Andante–Vif. The work, which takes six minutes to perform, is tonally unadventurous. It opens with sprightly rhythmic juxtapositions of the two instruments, in contrast to a later sweet and yielding melodic line. Even in this early work Poulenc, while learning much about rhythmic vivacity from Stravinsky, differs from his admired role model; while the Russian favoured fixed metrical rhythms, viewing music as an abstract art that expressed nothing, Poulenc was more sentimental, wanting music to portray a panoply of scenes and emotions, as had done past generations of

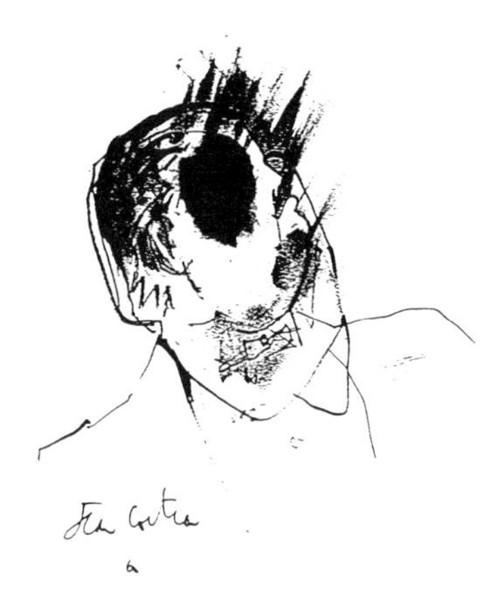

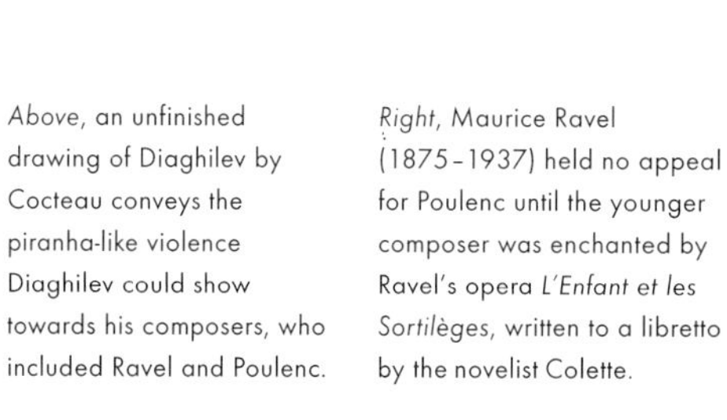

Above, an unfinished drawing of Diaghilev by Cocteau conveys the piranha-like violence Diaghilev could show towards his composers, who included Ravel and Poulenc.

Right, Maurice Ravel (1875–1937) held no appeal for Poulenc until the younger composer was enchanted by Ravel's opera *L'Enfant et les Sortilèges*, written to a libretto by the novelist Colette.

French composers from Rameau to Chabrier. The Sonata for two clarinets was later dismissed by Poulenc as 'childish stammering', a criticism which may have been specifically about the weak Andante, which is too obviously pianistic – its separate melodic lines are not written idiomatically for wind instruments but as if for two hands on a keyboard. Poulenc would continue to compose at the piano, but his idiomatic writing for wind instruments in future compositions would not betray this fact.

Another pleasant, but hardly significant, work was *Trois Mouvements perpétuels* (1918) for piano. Unlike a *moto perpetuo* in the Paganini tradition, Poulenc's idea of movement here was a brisk stroll by the Seine, to pleasant, animated sounds. The first movement is marked 'balanced, moderate' (Poulenc himself played it briskly, in forthright fashion), the second movement 'indifferently', then 'singingly'; only in the third movement, marked *alerte*, does the young composer wake up and show some of his mettle. The assertiveness of this section shows that Poulenc was indeed capable of breaking free from the bonds of fluent charm. Poulenc called the *Trois Mouvements perpétuels* 'ultra–easy', by which he may have been referring to the clear influence of Satie's spare, graceful *Gymnopédies*, with their touch of eighteenth-century simplicity. Lasting under five minutes, *Trois Mouvements* has a brevity typical of many of Poulenc's best early works. Their limpidity impressed Igor Stravinsky, who sent the pieces to Chester Music; they were then popularized by Ricardo Viñes, who programmed them in concert recitals across Europe.

This encouragement from his elders seemed justified when Poulenc's Sonata for piano duet was first heard in 1918. The new sonata had African-style savagery and Stravinskian percussiveness. It was divided into three movements, 'Prélude', 'Rustique' and 'Final' *(très vite)*. Fluency and facility were consciously avoided. The first movement, 'Prélude', opened with angular, rhythmically challenging keyboard attacks, and a certain restless uneasiness was evident in the pounding of the four hands, as if the two performers cohabited the same keyboard with difficulty. Although this sonata was no longer than the Sonata for two clarinets, it achieved more monumentality, partly because of the piano's percussive nature. The three-movement sonata form spun through Poulenc's three main musical influences:

Stravinsky in the first movement, Satie in the second, and Chabrier in the third. The first movement contains virtuoso display, much like Stravinsky's sometimes-violent piano works. The tension slackens in 'Rustique'; its naïve *andante,* almost like a nursery rhyme, is juxtaposed with trills, in the flavour of Satie's piano works. The 'Final' adds vigour but not melodic inspiration, although the tender charm that seeps through is reminiscent of Chabrier. Because this sonata was written for the composer to perform himself in company with another pianist (unlike the Sonata for two clarinets), it could express personal charm; sly rhythmic changes communicated bold wit, with seeming spontaneity and breeziness. The personality was attractive, and listeners wanted to hear more.

Among the first fans of the Sonata for piano duet was the conductor Ernest Ansermet, who wrote an enthusiastic article in *La Revue romande* in October 1919. Ansermet pointed out that Poulenc's sonata, rather than conforming to the standard sonata's thematic and harmonic development, presents three separate short pieces, distinct but hardly developed. Ansermet highlighted audible influences from Stravinsky, Ravel, Satie and Chabrier, but praised Poulenc's choice to limit himself to an 'apparent poverty' which argued musical discipline and restraint. Despite his many influences, the young composer dared to remain simple.

In the spring of 1917 Viñes proved helpful again, this time providing an introduction to Maurice Ravel, but when the adolescent Francis played piano for him, the elder man, in a contrary mood, stopped the boy. Poulenc kept his distance from Ravel thereafter, until he was enchanted by his opera, *L'Enfant et les Sortilèges* (1925). Poulenc never studied with Ravel, as shortly after their meeting Francis had to enter military service.

He was mobilized in January 1918 and did not enjoy his time in the services. He was rich, spoiled and glib, not a happy mixture of qualities for army service. At first he was based in Vincennes, outside Paris, as a 'non–instructed driver', but only a few months after induction, in May 1918, he found himself in military prison as a result of having over-stayed a leave in Paris. He wrote pathetic letters to friends to apprise them of the news. To Valentine Gross (who later married the artist Jean Hugo) Francis wailed, 'I must be helped ... I have great ideas in mind.' Even so, Francis did not lose his sense of humour, telling Valentine to spread the word among their friends about his jail experience, because it was 'so funny'.

While he was still serving his ten-day sentence, Francis received cheering letters from Jean Cocteau about a project to be called *Jongleurs* ('Jugglers') The work consisted of two movements, a raucous, violent *prélude* and a calm, classical principal movement. At first, Poulenc held *Jongleurs* in high esteem, calling it 'a thing of mad melancholy and of sensitivity unknown in my work until now'. Poulenc wanted the orchestration of the main movement to sound 'as clear as Mozart'. The *prélude* was a bit of wildness, or 'noise' as Poulenc called it, written for percussion instruments and 'Chinese one-note trumpets'. It was written at Cocteau's request for a stage performance, in 1919 and 1921; while *Jongleurs* was played, the well-known French dancer Caryathis moved with melancholy grace on stage. Not quite ballet music, *Jongleurs* was none the less inextricable from its theatrical context – hence Poulenc's later conviction that the, work had no independent musical value.

The presence of Chinese trumpets in *Jongleurs*'s *prélude* argues against the critic Renaud Machart's claim that it was 'the first piece for percussion alone in western music, predating Edgar Varèse's *Ionisation*'. Commentators have played down the influence of African music on Poulenc, largely because he often stated later in his career that he despised jazz. Nevertheless, in his early days as a composer, he was much influenced by Milhaud and Heitor Villa Lobos, both of whom were influenced by Afro-Brazilian culture.

Later, Poulenc would consciously try to suppress this vigorously rhythmic side of his youthful personality. As well as *Jongleurs* he destroyed a work which he had listed as his opus two after *Rapsodie nègre – Poèmes sénégalais*, also called *Quatre Chants sénégalais*. Poulenc decided that these wild new rhythms were not his true way, and that he could not follow the example of Varèse or other sound pioneers.

At this time Poulenc certainly wanted to appear original. He did not ask his friend Pablo Picasso to create the stage designs and costumes for *Jongleurs*, because he did not want his audience to be reminded of Satie's ballet *Parade*, for which Picasso's designs had made a strong impression. Francis did not want to seem to be copying his illustrious elders.

The self-critical composer destroyed other early works – a violin sonata 'in rag-time', a trio for piano, violin and cello, and a sonata for cimbalom and woodwind quartet. One work which did survive was a spoof song, written to a text by Cocteau, *Toréador*. Poulenc called it a 'hispano–italiano–french' song, since the toreador sings at length of his love for 'Pepita Queen of Venice' and bullfights on the Piazza San Marco. As one of the first songs by a great composer of French chanson, *Toréador* is a partial disappointment today. The thin joke is repetitious in Cocteau's poem, through twelve quatrains, and in addition a long refrain is repeated three times. (Poulenc's wider talent would be revealed in his aphoristic settings of Apolliniare's *Le Bestiaire*.) *Toréador* remains a unique case of overt *buffo* style in Poulenc's work, of holding forth in lengthy one-dimensional funniness. In later sly songs, set to Apollinaire or Max Jacob, Poulenc's humour would contain shades of melancholy or menace. The forced buffoonery of *Toréador* may have been an anticipation of the joy Francis would feel when he was released from the military in 1921. As a soldier he had been transferred frequently, but in the summer of 1919 he was finally given a secretarial post at the Air Ministry in Paris, arranged through connections.

During a military leave in Paris, Francis met Guillaume Apollinaire at the home of Valentine Hugo. The poet of *Alcools* and *Calligrammes* already had a considerable reputation, and not only as a poet. He was noted for his romantic liaisons, such as with the painter Marie Laurencin, a sometime lesbian. He had been accused of conspiring to steal the *Mona Lisa* from the Louvre; he had also managed to acquire a rare knowledge of arcane pornography from his role as cataloguer of the *enfer* section of the Bibliothèque nationale. His own efforts at writing pornography, such as the *Onze Mille Verges*, are sadistic exercises, full of ancient Chinese beheadings. Poulenc met Apollinaire again a few times before the poet's death in the 1918 Spanish flu epidemic, and registered 'that very special sound of his voice, half-ironic, half-melancholic. You'd think that all poets had soft, flat voices, for Apollinaire, like Eluard and Valéry, didn't make much noise.'

In 1918 Poulenc's bookseller friend Adrienne Monnier sent him a copy of the newly reprinted *Bestiaire*, which contained thirty poems and new woodcuts by Raoul Dufy (the published book begins with an eye-catching image of a muscular nude Orpheus). Poulenc often said that he identified his own musical art with the pictorial art of Dufy, and in his accounts of the birth of *Bestiaire*, he always mentioned the woodcuts. Visual stimulus was vital to Poulenc's musical inspiration.

The sober *Le Bestiaire* cycle, originally setting twelve songs, in its final form consisted of only six – 'Le Dromédaire' ('The Dromedary'), 'Le Chèvre du Thibet' ('The Tibetan Goat'), 'La Sauterelle' ('The Grasshopper'), 'Le Dauphin' ('The Dolphin'), 'L'Écrevisse' ('The Crayfish'), and 'La Carpe' ('The Carp'). These animals are identified

Guillaume Apollinaire (1880–1918) was a poet, pornographer and accused thief of the *Mona Lisa*. Poulenc was fascinated by his verse drama *Les Mamelles de Tirésias*, first performed at the time of World War I, and would later create an opera from it.

with a love story, and Apollinaire's philosophy of life is voiced in erudite, if concise, form. The verses are quatrains, as in the garrulous *Toréador*, but with each separate poem, the music changes mood, in a coherent, varied succession. The songs are so brief that they seem fleeting visions: as soon as the listener enters into the mood of one, it is already over, and the next has begun. Poulenc felt no unease about the brevity of the six songs: since childhood he had had on his music stand the example of Schoenberg's Six Little Piano Pieces, Op. 19 as a precedent for concentrated emotional statements.

The first song, 'Le Dromédaire' concerns the character Don Pedro d'Alfaroubeira, a medieval Infante of Portugal, who took dromedaries on a pilgrimage to the Holy Land. The music evokes the truculent march of a desert caravan. The heavy piano bass lurches along in slightly seasick fashion, cut off by a brisk skedaddling piano postlude, a childish pleasure when played with lightness and guilelessness by Poulenc himself. Neither weighty nor sprightly, the second song, 'Le Chèvre du Thibet', is a love song of melting tenderness, and its reference to the mythological Jason and The Golden Fleece obliges a singer to appear erudite as well as convincingly in love. Pierre Bernac, the incarnation of intelligence and sensitivity as a singer, had no problems here. The subject of the third song, 'La Sauterelle', would seem to invite hopping, energetic music, but Poulenc's music for a grasshopper is elegant, and even slower than the goat's love song. The melody sticks obstinately, even obsessively, to two notes, perhaps to evoke the monotony of insect life. 'Le Dauphin', about dolphins playing in the sea, is also written 'against' the text, in so far as the melody is melancholic (instead of leaping about sportively), accenting the fact that although dolphins play, 'life is still cruel.' The next song, 'L'Écrevisse', is more rapid in tempo, but its equally bittersweet message is that people, like crayfish, 'go ahead by moving backwards, ever backwards.' The movement of curling backwards is evoked with a sinuous melody that seems a sly reference to the 'desert' music for Don Pedro's camels that began *Le Bestiaire*. In the final song, even the continuity of life itself has an eerie, spooky quality for the carp in a swamp: 'Has death forgotten you, melancholy fish?' The piano part in 'La Carpe' suggests bells knolling ominously, as if asking for how long death will forget about the listener, as well as sounding a last echo of the swaying of Don Pedro's camels.

Opposite, Raoul Dufy at work on his giant wall painting, *La Fée Electricité*, for the Paris Exposition Universelle of 1937. Poulenc strongly identified with Dufy's work: the bright pastel colours and love of Paris evident in his paintings were also inspirations for some of Poulenc's music.

Throughout *Le Bestiaire* the vocal line is unforced and natural, sensitive to the accents and emphases of the French language. Yet unlike the raucous clowning of *Toréador*, *Le Bestiaire* has the innocence and gravity of a sad baby. Ravel's cycle *Histoires naturelles* based on long texts about animals by Jules Renard, may be seen as arch compared to *Le Bestiaire*; the latter is a truly intimate work. Rare are the modern works of music that have this aura of a private communication. That is why although a chamber orchestra version of *Bestiaire* exists, for string quartet, flute, clarinet, and bassoon, the simpler version for voice and piano is usually preferred.

On 8 June 1919, the art gallery dealer Léonce Rosenberg organized an afternoon in memory of Apollinaire, who had died the previous November. Among authors who read homages were Cocteau, André Breton, Blaise Cendrars, Max Jacob and Pierre Reverdy – a veritable 'who's who' of young French poets. But Poulenc described the event as 'something to put you to sleep', and to liven up the proceedings offered the première of his song cycle *Le Bestiaire*. For this performance at Rosenberg's gallery, Poulenc as pianist accompanied an Opéra-Comique soprano, Jeanne Borel. Although the work was well received, the composer said he would not have it performed again, as he felt the work's construction was faulty. He toyed with the idea of destroying the twelve short settings, but Raymonde Linossier and Georges Auric convinced him to cut the work in half. The remaining six songs, comprising a cycle lasting under five minutes, are as *Bestiaire* has become known to posterity. (Three of the *Bestiaire* songs that Poulenc had removed turned up later in his archives, 'La Puce', 'Le Serpent' and 'La Colombe'. They are not inferior to the songs which remained.)

Opposite, Jean Cocteau with a bust of his friend, the poet Anna de Noailles. A multi-talented poet, draughtsman, film-maker, stage designer and publicist, Cocteau dazzled the Paris cultural world, Poulenc included, for several decades.

The shorter *Bestiaire* was first performed by Poulenc with the soprano Suzanne Peignot, one of his closest musical allies. Another early interpreter was the Polish-born soprano Marya Freund, who sang at the world première of Schoenberg's *Gurrelieder* in Vienna in 1913. Freund sang local premières of the same composer's *Pierrot Lunaire* across Europe. Poulenc wrote, 'Only when Marya Freund sang *Le Bestiaire* as gravely as Schubert, did people realize it was better than a joke.' *Le Bestiaire* was praised by Ernest Ansermet and Igor Stravinsky and it has remained one of Poulenc's best-loved works.

A friend and fellow composer, Louis Durey, also made a vocal setting of Apollinaire's *Le Bestiaire* at the same time as Poulenc's, quite coincidentally. Durey waited until 1922 to have his *Bestiaire* performed by Jane Bathori. Jean Cocteau enjoyed both: 'Where Poulenc leaps with the paws of a young dog, Durey delicately poses his doe's feet. Both are natural, which is why we contemplate them with the same pleasure.' However, Durey's work is long forgotten.

At twenty and still in military uniform, Poulenc took a large step toward public renown. If he could later claim to be a misunderstood composer, he was never really an ignored one.

2

From Les Six to Les Biches 1920–24

Costume designs for Poulenc's ballet *Les Biches* by Marie Laurencin (1885–1956) subtly suggest sexual complexity: Laurencin showed women as romantic, seductive creatures who live on charm alone.

Diaghilev's idea was to stage a sort of modern Les Sylphides, *that is to say, a ballet of atmosphere. That's when I had the idea to place it in a vast room in a country house, with as the only furniture a vast sofa in Laurencin blue, modern* fêtes galantes. *About twenty flirtatious and ravishing women gamboled there with three handsome stalwarts dressed like oarsmen.*

Francis Poulenc, *Moi et mes amis*

From Les Six to Les Biches 1920–24

Opposite, never one to neglect a photo opportunity, Cocteau sent a collage version of a studio portrait of himself to many friends, including Poulenc. The result seems to be a self-conscious reference to the many artistic hats Cocteau was fond of wearing.

Sulking in military service, which would last until 1921, Poulenc knew that he would soon be able to rejoin his friends in the artistic ferment of post-war Paris. Music was swept along with the same energy that created such post-World War I artistic movements as Dada, Cubism and Surrealism. Darius Milhaud travelled to Brazil in January 1917 as secretary to the poet-diplomat Paul Claudel and returned towards the end of 1918 with a suitcase full of samba rhythms. These went into such masterpieces as the ballets *Le Boeuf sur le toit* (1919) and *La Création du monde* (1923). All one needed, it seemed, was a bunch of vibrant friends and a manifesto. Poulenc had both.

In 1920 in Paris, a group of young musicians enjoyed dining together and going to music halls. They all knew the poet Jean Cocteau, a publicist for everyone from a transvestite tightrope walker, Barbette, to a drugged black-American boxer, his lover, 'Panama' Al Brown. Cocteau promoted his young musician friends as an alternative to the conservative Schola Cantorum, which taught religious music in the tradition of César Franck and Vincent d'Indy. He urged listeners to escape from pious, heavy-going concerts and listen to life-enhancing works; music, according to the hyperactive young poet, was not meant to be heard 'with your head in your hands'.

The emaciated Cocteau whirled through life like an overgroomed, opiated poodle, irritating as many people as he astonished. Even Poulenc, a friend since 1917, took some decades before his eyes could focus on Cocteau's speed-of-light activities. His major settings of Cocteau's texts, *La Voix humaine* and *La Dame de Monte Carlo*, would not be written until forty years later, but, even then, Poulenc preferred not to set Cocteau's poems, believing that they were closer in spirit to films or to the theatre than to the chanson.

After concocting the general idea for the Ballets Russes spectacle *Parade* in 1917, with décors by Picasso and music by Satie, Cocteau pursued his ideals in a book, *Le Coq et L'Arlequin*, a bunch of singular

à Francis Poulenc
souvenir
de Londres Jean Cocteau
HANA STUDIOS L^TD
22, BEDFORD ST STRAND,
LONDON.

opinions about music by a non-musician. Cocteau attacked Wagner and disliked the 'Russian influence', which Poulenc, a great admirer of Mussorgsky, would hardly have agreed with; he even attacked the later works of Debussy, which Poulenc adored. Cocteau did, however, like Erik Satie, above all, for his simplicity. Most of Poulenc's friends also admired Satie's pared-down, spooky music. His *Socrate* (1920), written for two sopranos and a small chamber ensemble, was described by the composer Henri Sauguet as, being 'like a reading of the Gospels in Gregorian chant'. Satie created works destined to retain their strangeness forever, solemn but not weighty, serious but not solid. Daring to be weird and to follow his aesthetic urge was second nature to Satie. He collected umbrellas obsessively, and after his death dozens of them, most still in their wrappers, were discovered crowded together in his miniscule suburban apartment.

For young composers like Poulenc and Milhaud, Satie's refusal to conform served as an example of how not to be a nice boy in music. Satie, capable of charm in his *Gymnopédies*, also pointed out moments when charm should be avoided. Unfortunately, as the 1920s progressed, his artistic and emotional control dissipated through illness brought on by alcoholism. The young members of Les Six looked with dismay at Satie's tantrums and his weaker works that followed *Parade* and *Socrate*.

In January 1920 the music critic and composer Henri Collet wrote an article in *Comœdia* entitled, 'Les Cinq Russes, les Six Français, et Satie'. Collet declared that after the nineteenth-century Russian musical group known as The Five (Balakirev, Borodin, Cui, Mussorgsky and Rimsky-Korsakov), France went one better in having Les Six. Darius Milhaud recalled:

[Collet] chose six names absolutely arbitrarily, those of Auric, Durey, Honegger, Poulenc, Tailleferre and me simply because we knew each other and we were pals and appeared on the same musical programmes, no matter if our temperaments and personalities weren't at all the same! Auric and Poulenc followed some ideas of Cocteau, Honegger followed German Romanticism, and myself, Mediterranean lyricism!

Contrary to contemporary notions held about the light-spirited attitude of the group, at least one of Les Six, Arthur Honegger, loved

A portrait of Cocteau and Les Six from 1922: from left, Milhaud, Cocteau, Honegger, Tailleferre, Poulenc and Durey. Georges Auric being absent, Cocteau hastily sketched a portrait of the missing friend.

the heavy religious music that Cocteau claimed his friends were trying to abandon; Poulenc would also compose serious religious works.

This eclectic group, announced in 1920, did not last longer than 1921, when the eldest of them, Louis Durey, left his friends to live in Saint-Tropez. Durey's left-wing views distanced him from the high-society salons that advanced the careers of Poulenc and Auric, and to this day his music remains unrecorded and largely unpublished. Poulenc and Milhaud are the most admired and performed today, followed by Honegger. Auric is remembered mostly as a film composer (the 'Moulin Rouge waltz' from the José Ferrer film *Moulin Rouge* being his greatest hit) and Germaine Tailleferre, the only woman of the group, is perhaps the most forgotten of all.

Continuing interest in Les Six may lie less with their artistic posterity than with nostalgia for their qualities of youth and energy – Les Six should never have grown old. It is poignant to see photographs of reunions of Les Six thirty years on – a sexagenarian Cocteau looking like a mangy tiger with a facelift, Milhaud obese and immobile in a wheelchair, Tailleferre like a dumpy retired public-school principal – for a moment, these musicians had the charisma of youth and enjoyed it deeply.

Poulenc contributed to the Les Six sensibility by writing racy dancing tunes inspired by popular music he had heard by the banks of the Marne River when visiting his grandparents at Nogent. A key work created just before the 'formation' of Les Six was Poulenc's setting in 1919 of three texts by Jean Cocteau, *Cocardes*. The three songs are 'Miel de Narbonne', 'Bonne d'Enfant', and 'Enfant de troupe'. Nonsense texts create a brittle scenario: 'Polka … soft caramels, acidulous bonbons … Hamburg … Bock … strawberry syrup'. In its tawdry fairground atmosphere *Cocardes* musically resembles Satie's *Parade*. Poulenc's raucous orchestral writing, for brass, drum, violin, and triangle – creating what he termed a *fête foraine* (fun fair) sound – was in key with other works by friends, like Milhaud's *Le Boeuf sur le toit* and Auric's *Foxtrot*. Whereas *Le Bestiaire* consisted of emotional miniatures with a heartfelt message, *Cocardes* breezed by, satisfied with

Above, Cocteau and Auric in 1924, a year after the death of Cocteau's lover, the novelist Raymond Radiguet (1903–23), also a great friend of Auric. Cocteau has the faraway stare of an opium addict, which he indeed became after Radiguet's death. *Right*, a scene of calmer happiness is Milhaud and Poulenc in 1921, in Milhaud's home town of Aix-en-Provence.

a simple evocation of the atmosphere of a fairground. Poulenc claimed that his main influence for this work was not musical but visual, that of the brightly coloured patriotic canvases of a friend, Roger de la Fresnaye.

The funny, sophisticated music of *Cocardes* is what we have come to think of as typical of Les Six (who felt a sincere sympathy for popular music). Heartlessly comic, even satirical, it visits the popular idiom of fairground music and mechanical pianos; Cocteau and Poulenc considered *Cocardes* as an act of homage to the *bal musette*. Yet these witty creators, observing a working man dancing with his sweetheart, could never belong to such an event because of their social class, education or, in some cases, sexuality. When Poulenc and Cocteau visited a popular milieu, they were like Marcel Proust among the butcher boys.

The friends gave concerts in an artist's studio, on the rue Huyghens in the fourteenth arrondissement, equipped with a smelly heating system and hard wooden benches. Fashionable folk flocked to hear trendy new sounds. At the first Les Six concert to feature foreign composers, works by Bartók and Schoenberg were performed, as well as music by Lord Berners, Arthur Lourié and Alfredo Casella. Guests included the pianist Marcelle Meyer, the painter Marie Laurencin, Cocteau's lover Raymond Radiguet and Proust's friend Lucien Daudet.

Soon the festivities attracted a snobby society crowd. A number of these rich hangers-on sponsored artistic activities: one of them was the Comte Etienne de Beaumont, a party-giver who commissioned Satie's ballet *Mercure* and Milhaud's *Salade*. Other wealthy members of the Cocteau crowd dabbled in music. Yvonne, Marquise de Casa Fuerte studied violin at the Paris Conservatoire and in 1931 founded a new music group, La Sérénade. Poulenc referred to the Marquise as 'the sweetest swallow of springtime'. When an evening of Les Six music was presented at the Comédie des Champs-Elysées theatre in February 1921, the Comte Etienne de Beaumont bought the best seats for his friends. The Shah of Persia paid dearly for a seat from which he could see nothing, but from where he could be seen by all. A popular impression grew of Les Six as silly, carnival-loving musicians, and this reputation has stuck to Poulenc to this day. On 18 June 1921 the ballet *Les Mariés de la Tour Eiffel* was presented at the Théâtre des Champs-

Impresario Rolf de Maré (1888–1964) produced the shows of his Ballets Suédois from his office at Paris's Théâtre des Champs-Elysées; these included the famous ballet *Les Mariés de la Tour Eiffel* (1921), in which the composers of Les Six collaborated.

Elysées. Rolf de Maré, director of the Ballets Suédois (Swedish Ballet), had asked Georges Auric to write a score for him, but Auric was short of musical ideas and asked his composer friends to bail him out. *Les Mariés* tried to confer a childlike poetry on everyday aspects of Paris life, which included the Eiffel Tower, press photographers, the gramophone and cyclists. Louis Durey withdrew from the project, hating Cocteau's disrespect towards Ravel. Poulenc and Tailleferre filled in at the last minute with hastily written pieces. Poulenc contributed a polka with a languid waltz passage, *La Baigneuse de Trouville*, and a comic *Discours du général* (a revenge for his military miseries); they were Poulenc's first tentative orchestral pieces.

Les Mariés shows the great difference in aesthetic of each member of the group. When performed today, the work is long and tedious, particularly the texts by Cocteau. In 1923 Poulenc was to say that apart from Auric's overture, 'it's still shit'. Yet the frenzied atmosphere of *Les Mariés* faithfully evokes the party which Poulenc's life had become. In the evenings he indulged in 'cocktails and recocktails' and one night he performed a dance wearing only pyjama bottoms which he had taken off by the end of the dance. 'It was pretty, so pretty!' recalled Louis Durey. Cocteau related the same wild party: 'Poulenc completely naked. Valentine [Hugo] dying of fear that her maid would be scandalized. Poulenc as comfortable as if he were wearing a monk's cowl.'

When the parties were over, Francis showed signs of youthful uncertainty as a composer, and on his final release from military duties in January 1921 he felt obliged to excel musically. He wrote four songs to poems by Max Jacob, for his beloved *fête foraine* ensemble (voice and flute, clarinet, oboe, bassoon and trumpet), but destroyed them shortly after the first performance in January 1922. The songs betray a certain complexity for its own sake, with difficult changes in rhythm that seem uncalled for. In these early songs Poulenc may have been tempted to imitate the intellectual rigour of works he admired by Stravinsky and Schoenberg, instead of remaining simple and direct as was his wont. Milhaud, the dedicatee, saved a manuscript of these songs (they are to be published shortly by Salabert Editions in Paris). Poulenc also destroyed a *Caprice espagnol* for oboe and piano written the same year, and a large work, *Marches militaires*, for piano and orchestra, which he worked on for several years. A frenzy of self-censorship also affected a collaborative work with Cocteau, *Le Gendarme incompris* ('The Misunderstood Bobby'), a piece which when performed in May 1921 was billed as a *critique-bouffe*. A policeman spouted lines from a prose-poem by Mallarmé to saucy music by Poulenc, which he later destroyed, although a copy of it was discovered and published in 1988 by Salabert Editions. The score consists of an overture, four interludes and a finale written for voice and chamber orchestra, consisting of double bass, cello, violin, clarinet, trumpet, trombone and drums – the same type of *fête foraine* sound as in *Cocardes*. A July 1921 performance in London of *Le Gendarme incompris* conducted by Ernest Ansermet was booed: the audience thought that Poulenc was a student of the then much-despised Stravinsky.

Among the audience at *Le Gendarme incompris* was the influential Misia Sert, Diaghilev's closest woman friend and a talent scout for the

Ballets Russes. Misia was a muse for painters including Pierre Bonnard and Édouard Vuillard, and claimed to have discovered Coco Chanel. She had invited Poulenc to her Paris salon in 1919 following reports of his talent from Ricardo Viñes and decided that here was a composing talent fit for Diaghilev; soon Poulenc was to hear from the ballet impresario himself.

Despite his self-censoriousness, Francis had a reputation for being prolific and facile. In 1921 Auric snarled that he was not 'like Poulenc or Milhaud, capable of writing any old thing any old time'. All of Les Six were equally merciless about each other's work. When Honegger's cantata *Le Roi David* had its first performance in 1921, Poulenc dismissed the work as 'very *boche*–Swiss–ridiculous'. Poulenc's overall immediate public success, however, made it seem as if he had it easy. In 1921 he told the Belgian pianist and musicologist Paul Collaer, 'Belgian critics find me "agreeable, charming". They should look out, one never knows which acrid odours, chemically combined, produce the rose's perfume.' The reference to chemical transformation suggested that he was more like Mr Hyde than Dr Jekyll. Poulenc clearly wanted to seem as subversive in art as his master, Erik Satie.

Cocteau's splashy public events made the young Francis self-conscious about his image. He was also acutely aware that he had much to learn as a composer; in comparison to his idol Stravinsky he lacked secure notions of musical architecture, development and counterpoint. Poulenc's phase of complexity for its own sake in the *Quatres Poèmes de Max Jacob* may have been a danger signal to him. Since the route to the Conservatoire was barred, Poulenc followed Milhaud's advice and went to see the composer Charles Koechlin, a renowned teacher of counterpoint whose orchestration skills were widely respected. (In 1898 Gabriel Fauré had asked Koechlin to orchestrate his stage music for *Pelléas et Mélisande.*) A jovial, if impoverished, composer with a Neptune beard, Koechlin had a righteous streak, but was flexible with his students. Poulenc got off to a poor start in his first letter to the master by spelling his name wrong – Koecklin. The teacher soon realized that tedious counterpoint exercises were not the thing for Poulenc so he asked the young man to work instead on harmony, instructing him to write several four-part chorales each week, based on chorale melodies of J. S. Bach. These weekly exercises were to help Poulenc later when he composed *a cappella* vocal works.

The first fruit of this study was the riotous chorus, *Chanson à boire* (1922), written to an anonymous seventeenth-century text. Complete with belches and vomiting in the best part-song tradition, the work was composed for a member of the Harvard Glee Club whom Poulenc had met in Paris. Ultimately, it was banned from public performance in the USA because of Prohibition laws. *Chanson à boire* is good solid theatre, with its protestation of 'I'll drink no more, wah-wah-wah!' Years later Poulenc confessed his admiration for this early effort, which began 'rather like drunken Orlando de Lassus, but don't accent the *suce* [suck] when you talk about me'. Despite its unpretentious gaiety, *Chanson à boire* fits into the tradition of Franco–Flemish vocal polyphony, in its clarity in the combined vocal textures and attention to the meaning of words that were set.

Poulenc continued to produce minor piano works for his friends Marcelle Meyer and Ricardo Viñes to perform, and, in 1922, marking the beginning of a return to the clarity and simplicity of his first works and a move away from the fruitless quest for complexity, Poulenc wrote two sonatas, one for clarinet and bassoon and another for horn, trumpet and trombone. The Sonata for clarinet and bassoon was more confident than the Sonata for two clarinets of 1918, a reflection of Poulenc's greater understanding of the way in which the two instruments differ and how they blend. The work is a two-way monologue as opposed to a dialogue, rather like a married couple, each with a conflicting version of an event. The work is divided into three movements: an Allegro with staccato accents, a sweet-sounding Romance played *andante*, and a Finale which Poulenc marked 'very animated'. In the second and third movements particularly, the clarinet takes the melodic lead as the incarnation of romance. The typical movement structure of the classical sonata – fast–slow–fast – is a return to the example set by the Sonata for two clarinets. By contrast, the Sonata for horn, trumpet and trombone is more extrovert, like a beer-garden polka. The first movement, Allegro moderato, is marked *gracioso*. The trumpet leads with a theme in folk-song style that seems to prefigure his future ballet *Les Biches*. As in many other works from this period, Poulenc aspired to an eighteenth-century

During a tour to Salzburg in August 1922 for the International Chamber Music Festival, Poulenc developed a surprising crush on Anton von Webern (1882–1945). Webern, shown here a decade later, rarely inspired lust in his listeners.

clarity but with the energy of a circus band. A second movement, Andante, marked 'very slow', and an 'animated' Rondeau end the piece with graceful simplicity. Poulenc later described this sonata as being brightly coloured, like the canvases of Raoul Dufy.

The Sonata for clarinet and bassoon and the Sonata for horn, trumpet and trombone were both written at the time that Poulenc began lessons in composition with Koechlin. It is natural to wonder to what extent the improvement between these 1922 works and the Sonata for two clarinets (1918) was due to Koechlin's teaching. In fact, Poulenc remained very much a self-starter. On his own he studied treatises on harmony by Henri Reber and on wind instruments by Gabriel Parès. Poulenc sought practical advice not just from Koechlin, but also from Albert Roussel and Nadia Boulanger. Thus his sources of information and influences remained diverse.

In 1922, to satisfy their curiosity about new music, Poulenc and Milhaud travelled to Vienna with Marya Freund, who presented them to Arnold Schoenberg. At Alma Mahler's house, they met Alban Berg and Anton von Webern, and Poulenc had his photograph taken with Schoenberg. The resulting image is such an unlikely juxtaposition and the two men look so happy in one another's presence that it resembles a photo-montage. The friendly welcome encountered in Vienna says much about the open-mindedness of the musicians of the city.

In August of the same year Poulenc met Webern again at an International Festival of Chamber Music in Salzburg, and described him as 'an exquisite boy', probably the first and last time that Webern was so termed. Poulenc also found Webern's string quartet 'adorable', and clearly regarded his music as an exquisite collector's item, like a Chinese lacquered box, as well as admiring the appearance of the fine-featured if mousy man. Poulenc recognized in Webern an ability to master a musical language and it was this that lent Webern's music the authenticity that was of utmost importance to Poulenc. He also had purely musical concerns during the visit: he complained to the Salzburg committee that they had omitted from the festival works by Satie, Auric and Prokofiev. He sent Milhaud a graded report of the composers played at the Festival, rating them from +20 to -20. They included: Richard Strauss (12), Milhaud (18), Joseph Marx (8), Arthur Bliss (-11), Bartók (18), Malipiero (2), Poulenc (13), Stravinsky (14), Debussy (10), Koechlin (15), Granados (5), Falla (16), Honegger (10), Nielsen (-4), Ravel (-11), Busoni (-15), Szymanowski (-2), Webern (19), Hindemith (13), Ethel Smyth (8), Kodály (14). The highest marks were given to Webern, and the lowest to someone named Wilhelm Grosz (-20), whose concert was described as follows: 'abominable, packed house, shameful, enemy of Webern.'

Another trip with Milhaud in 1923 to southern Italy inspired pale piano pieces that included *Napoli* (1925), a three-part work. Despite its favour with performers like Claudio Arrau and Arthur Rubinstein, Poulenc despised *Napoli*. His voyages, however, would soon cease as he began serious work. In response to Misia Sert's enthusiasm, in 1921 Diaghilev had asked Poulenc for a ballet score, which became *Les Biches*. Poulenc approached the task slowly but methodically; like a boxer preparing for a title bout, he trained for the challenge of writing an 'opéra ballet bouffe'. He read scores by Verdi and Rossini and was struck by the 'great masterpiece' *Rigoletto*, especially Gilda's aria 'Caro nome'. He studied Rimsky-Korsakov's treatise on orchestration and took extra lessons with Koechlin. In the meantime he worked on a string quartet, which he later destroyed; he admitted to 'detesting' string quartets, but had wanted to see if he could manage to arrive at something unusual.

Les Biches remains one of Poulenc's most famous works, partly because Diaghilev and the Ballets Russes have entered the realm of myth. Since Poulenc was no Apollo, he was not harassed by Diaghilev's sexual attention, and he revelled in the atmosphere of Byzantine gossip that surrounded the impresario and his court. When Germaine Tailleferre fell in love with the noted violinist Jacques Thibaud, himself in love with a famous soprano, Poulenc could not stop gossiping: he was in his element.

Diaghilev had wanted *Les Biches* finished in six months but the composer took his time, and its première was not given until January 1924 in Monte Carlo. Poulenc relished his role as promising young composer of whom wonders were expected. Fun was everywhere. He used silly nicknames for friends: Darius Milhaud was 'fat Da'; the distinguished critic Henry Pruniers was 'Pruneton' (Big Plum), 'Pruneprune,' or the feminine 'Pruneline'; another critic, Bernard Gavoty, was dubbed the positively female 'La Gavotte.' Francis signed his letters 'Poupoule' or 'Poulet' (chicken). Insouciance was an integral part of Poulenc's 1920s.

Some Poulenc enthusiasts are seduced by the atmosphere of the Diaghilev Ballets Russes and the ballet's fame; others criticize the score as not one of Poulenc's most accomplished. Both views are correct. *Les Biches* is a suite of dance movements and choral interludes about nothing in particular. On stage, sixteen lovely young women were courted by three athletes in rowing costumes. The evanescence of the pleasures shown on stage is part of the poignancy of *Les Biches*; and the emotional climate has much in common with the best works of the eighteenth-century painter Antoine Watteau, whose scenes of revellers aware of swiftly passing time much appealed to Poulenc. *Les Biches* is above all dance music – with neo-classical charm – its elegant scoring for wind instruments is as delicate as that of Gounod or Tchaikovsky; in fact, Poulenc borrowed a melody from Tchaikovsky's *Sleeping Beauty* for his graceful Adagietto. The choral interludes, inspired by Stravinsky's folkloric works like *Les Noces*, *Renard* and

Opposite, Cocteau produced drawings in the way that other people doodle and his letters to Poulenc teem with visual imaginings that complement the breathless, affectionate messages from poet to composer.

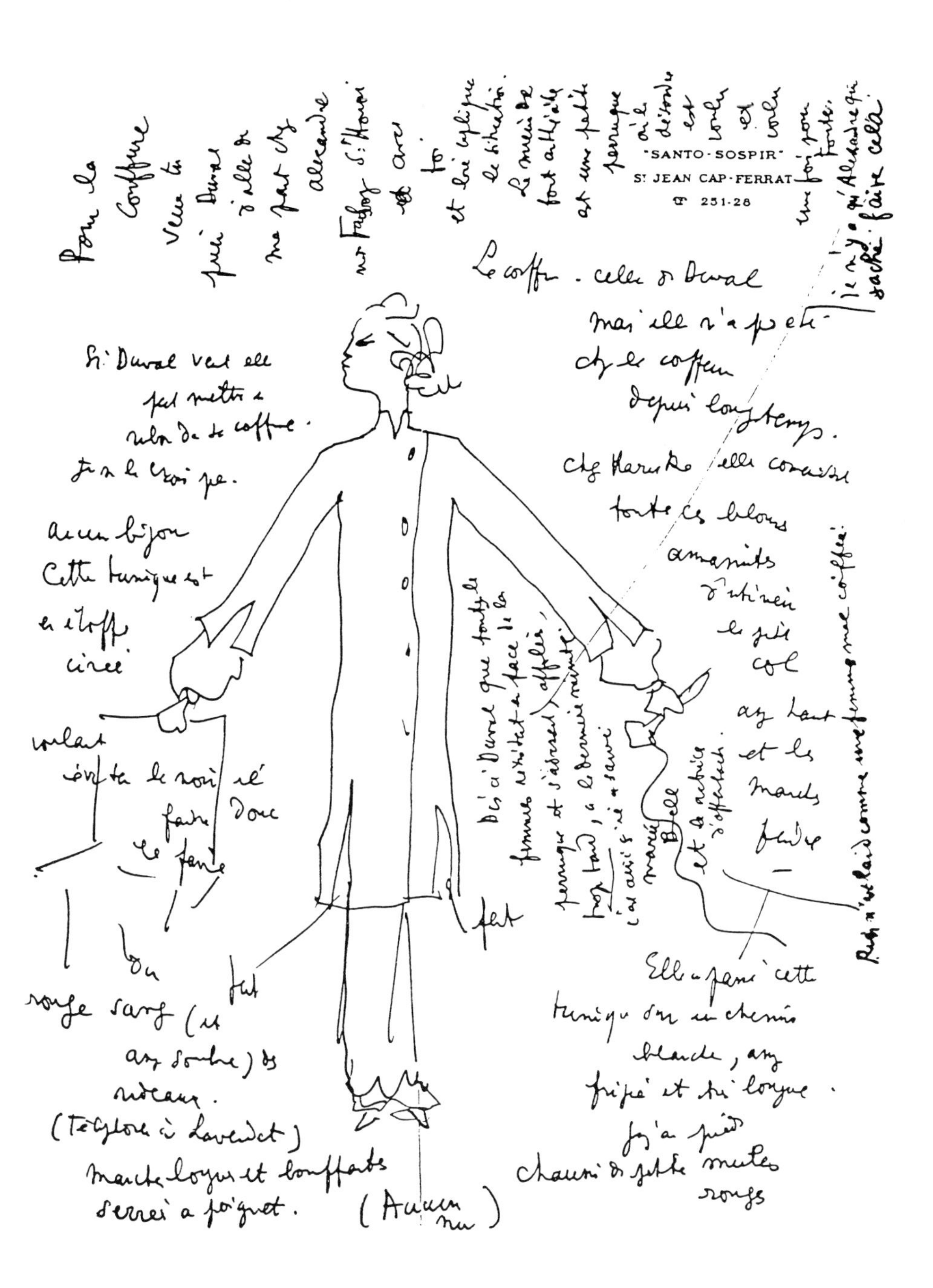
"SANTO-SOSPIR"
ST JEAN CAP-FERRAT
251-28
aucun bijou
Cette tunique est en étoffe cirée

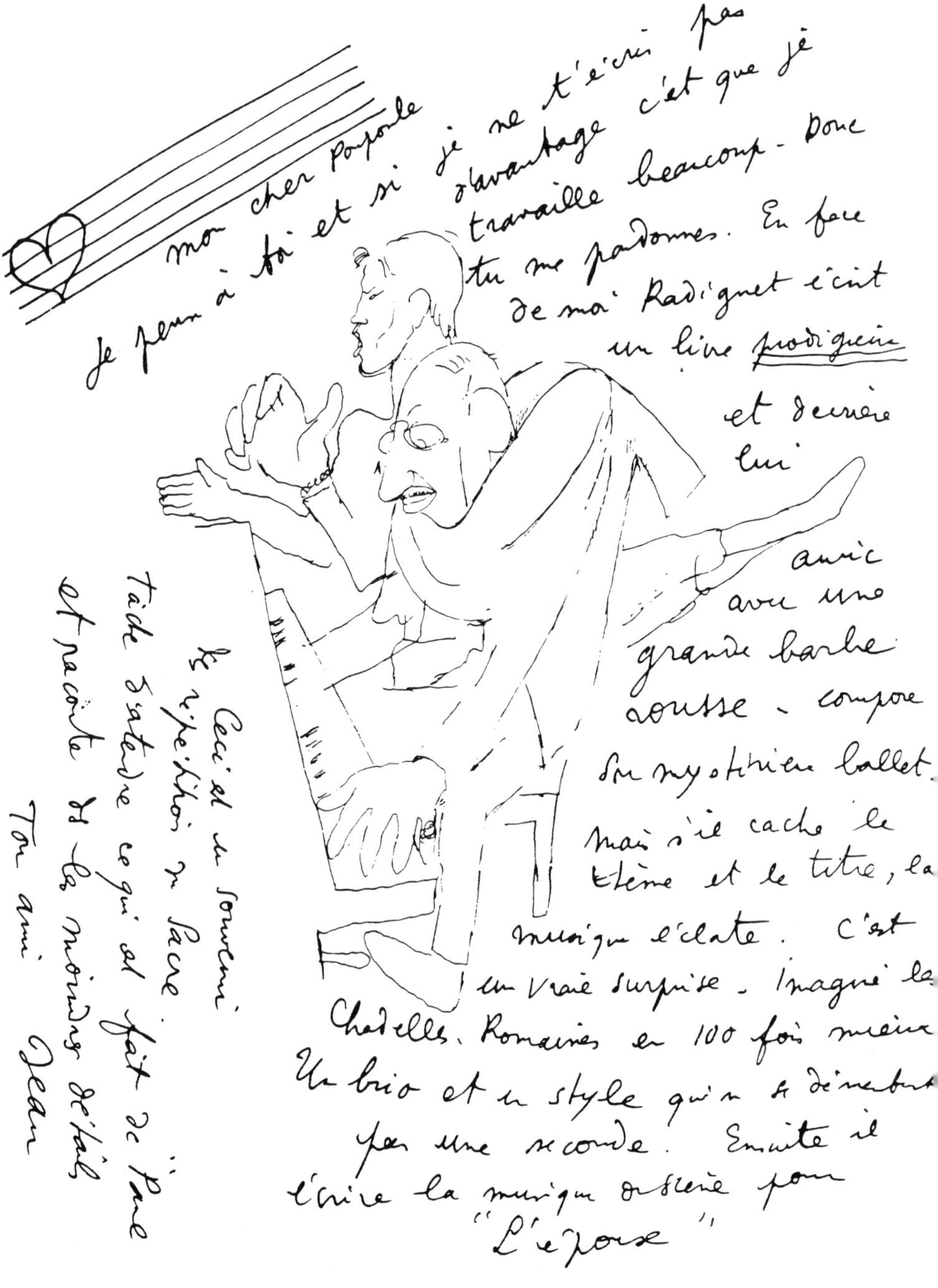

Mon cher Poupoule

Je pense à toi et si je ne t'écris pas davantage c'est que je travaille beaucoup. Donc tu me pardonnes. En face de moi Radiguet écrit un livre prodigieux

et derrière lui

Auric avec une grande barbe rousse compose son mystérieux ballet. Mais s'il cache le thème et le titre, la musique éclate. C'est une vraie surprise. Imagine les Chapelles Romaines en 100 fois mieux. Un brio et un style qui ne se démentent pas une seconde. Ensuite il écrira la musique de scène pour "L'épouse"

Le Cecil est un souvenir.
L'expédition me sacre.
Tâche d'attendre ce qui est fait de pire
et raconte moi les moindres détails
Ton ami Jean

Opposite, an illustrated letter from July 1922 from Cocteau to Poulenc, his 'cher Poupoule'; the drawing shows Stravinsky and Nijinsky at the piano, at a rehearsal of *The Rite of Spring*.
Below, the peekaboo sexuality evident in the stage costumes by Marie Laurencin for Poulenc's ballet *Les Biches* is well illustrated here, where the fox's garment might also appear to be the animal's genitalia.

Pulcinella, are less convincing. Poulenc's folklore sounds forced and imported in his first efforts in choral writing with orchestra; he would improve quickly. (Milhaud, in his ballets *Salade* and *L'Homme et son désir*, was also inspired by Stravinsky's choral interludes.)

Les Biches is most often heard today in the form of an orchestral suite. Instead of the nine original movements, Poulenc omitted the overture and three choral movements in the five-movement suite, made up of Rondeau, Adagietto, Rag-Mazurka, Andantino and Final. These titles are evocative rather than being exact descriptions of musical content. The Rondeau in *Les Biches* is not technically a rondo, as that musical term is usually defined (a refrain recurs throughout the piece); nor does the Rag-Mazurka contain a mazurka in the Chopin tradition. Poulenc's mazurka is closer to a Sicilian tarantella, and the Rag section was inspired rhythmically by Stravinsky's *Ragtime*. As was often the case with his works, Poulenc kept retouching the orchestration of *Les Biches*. Only in 1940 was he willing to let well enough alone, and the ballet and the suite acquired their final forms. Henri Sauguet noted that *Les Biches* was 'more instrumented than orchestrated', meaning that the instruments played as individual voices rather than forming part of a collective mass of sound.

Poulenc felt at home in Laurencin's designs for *Les Biches*, a wonder-world of graceful animals and young, but erotically sophisticated maidens. The phallic straining neck of the horse is juxtaposed with the girl's face, prettily insipid.

Two great British dancers who adopted exotic-sounding stage names to make international careers, Alicia Markova and Anton 'Pat' Dolin, participated in 1930s London performances of *Les Biches*, retitled in English *The House Party*. Here they are photographed in rehearsal, *far right*, in performance.

The question of influence in Poulenc's work is far from clear. Stravinsky, who was a great inspiration to Poulenc, admitted to being influenced by Tchaikovsky and Gounod. So was Poulenc influenced directly by Gounod and Tchaikovsky, or through the example set by Stravinsky? This sort of question distracts from what was very much a work composed on the pleasure principle. It was not only the melodies of other composers that influenced Poulenc, but also their rhythms: while writing music, he would spend hours at the piano, thumping out the scores of operas, from Weber's *Der Freischütz* to Mozart's *Don Giovanni*. By these means he would find rhythms and would change the tunes to fit his needs. One example is the section 'Jeu' in *Les Biches*, in which the orchestra plays a variation of the aria 'Je suis brésilien, j'ai de l'or' from Offenbach's *La Vie parisienne*. Poulenc's Rag-Mazurka movement in *Les Biches* contains another

example, a setting to the rhythm of the comic quintet from Bizet's *Carmen.*

Despite, or perhaps because of these borrowings and inspirations, *Les Biches* is fresh and charming. Even if the Adagietto were originally written by Tchaikovsky, it still fits perfectly into Poulenc's work and has the lyric sweep of his best melodies. For Poulenc, *Les Biches* was in artistic unity with the ballet's softly feminine décor, designed by Marie Laurencin, and its coy choreography by Bronislava Nijinska, Nijinsky's sister. Despite the heterosexual aura to the ballet, there was also a subtle scene of lesbian romance. The critic Boris de Schloezer said that the work's 'very personal spirit ... its grace, naïvety and slight perversity, its sentimental and sensual erotism ... belong especially to Poulenc.'

The success of *Les Biches* broke up Poulenc's friendship with Erik Satie. One of the most enthusiastic critics of *Les Biches* and Auric's ballet, *Les Fâcheux*, was Louis Laloy. The critic was on bad terms with Satie, because of Satie's stormy relationship with the late Claude Debussy, a great friend of Laloy. Satie scolded the young composers about the praise they received from Laloy, and left Monte Carlo in a huff, standing all the way in the train back to Paris. Once there, he wrote articles calling the ballets by Poulenc and Auric 'musical lemonade'. In response, they sent Satie a child's rattle that Poulenc had found in a toyshop, with a white-bearded head that resembled Satie. The old composer was so furious that even on his deathbed he refused to see Poulenc or Auric. 'What's the use of seeing them again?' asked the dying man. 'Debussy died, without my seeing *him* again.'

Poulenc's unclouded friendship with Manuel de Falla made up for his strife with Satie. He had first met Falla at the home of Viñes in 1918 and admired the Spaniard's intense spirituality: 'Falla was a mystic in the pure state of the term ... like a block of crystal.' Poulenc had intended to dedicate his *Caprice espagnol* for oboe and piano, later destroyed, to Falla. But when Poulenc would finally finish his trio for piano, oboe, and bassoon, in 1926, it was published with the promised dedication to Falla, 'to prove my tender admiration'.

Capable of unlimited admiration for his musical idols, Poulenc could also feel boundless contempt for others. In his correspondence there spring up testy anti-Semitic references directed at a rival

Manuel de Falla (1876–1946), pictured in 1926, was greatly admired by Poulenc – but the ascetic Spaniard, given to migraines and religious self-torment, refused to see Poulenc when the Frenchman planned to visit him in Spain.

composer, Maxime Jacob (not to be confused with the poet Max Jacob, Poulenc's friend). Poulenc called Jacob 'a little no-talent plagiarist jew', and some days later, he spoke of the music publisher Eschig as 'the Jew from the rue de Rome'. Although Poulenc later admitted he was never 'philosemite', solid friendships with Jewish artists like Darius Milhaud usually kept such reflections in check. Poulenc's few comments never translated into actions against Jews, unlike other French musicians. Francis's beloved teacher Viñes was a rabid anti-Dreyfusard at the beginning of the century, and Poulenc might have followed him in that direction if it were not that Vincent d'Indy, an extreme anti-Semite and a strong supporter of the government in the Dreyfus case, was anathema to them both.

These unattractive comments in 1923 point to a period of stress after the completion of *Les Biches*, compounded by the shocking death from typhoid fever of the twenty-year-old novelist Raymond Radiguet, Cocteau's lover. A dramatic telegram arrived at Monte Carlo, where Poulenc was preparing the première of his ballet: 'Radiguet died last night. Poor Jean frightful state. Darius.' Poulenc could not leave rehearsals to attend the funeral. He said, 'For two days I was unable to do anything, I was so stunned.' Yet two weeks later he was telling jokes to Diaghilev about a male ballet dancer named Koscov, who 'still seems to have a very warmed-up ass. I helped him do pirouettes this morning.'

For the moment, Poulenc was resilient and artistically fulfilled. Death was still a distant threat.

3

Transformations 1925–35

Poulenc at the piano with his harpsichordist friend Wanda Landowska. She commissioned Poulenc's *Concert champêtre* and encouraged his first homosexual relationship with the painter Richard Chanlaire.

It would be totally unfair if I didn't speak here about a home belonging to Marie-Laure de Noailles, where I composed Aubade. *There I also played countless times new works for Auric, Jacques Février, and most recently,* Figure humaine *to Picasso and Paul Eluard. Only, because of Marie-Laure's extraordinary knowledge of painting, her apartment at the place des États-Unis symbolizes painting for me – and God knows I love paintings – while the home of Marie-Blanche de Polignac on the rue Barbet-de-Jouy is for me the home of music. One, Marie-Laure, speaks to me of Antonello da Messina like an old friend. The other, Marie-Blanche de Polignac, speaks of Monteverdi as of a living musician.*

Francis Poulenc, *Journal de mes mélodies*

Transformations 1925–35

In 1924 the magazine *La Révue musicale* commissioned eight prominent composers to write songs to texts by the sixteenth-century poet Pierre de Ronsard. Poulenc was not among the group of composers who were asked; it included elders he despised, like Maurice Ravel, Paul Dukas, Maurice Delage, and André Caplet, and contemporaries whose music he did not like either, Arthur Honegger and Roland-Manuel. Reacting with pique to his own exclusion from this project, Poulenc produced five settings of Ronsard poems. He liked to say that the best thing about the Ronsard songs was the Picasso drawing printed on the cover, and he dunned the artist to provide a drawing of a guitar in time for the printing deadline. While doing so, he poured venom into Picasso's ear about his artistic enemies, such as Georges Braque. He also dished the dirt about Diaghilev, telling Picasso that he had helped the Russian discover a young Spanish composer, possibly Salvador Bacarisse, who was 'talented, twenty-five, and has a pretty body. You can imagine Serge's joy.'

Poulenc's *Cinq Poèmes de Ronsard* are settings of 'Attributs', 'Le Tombeau', 'Ballet', 'Je n'ai plus que les os' ('I am nothing but bones') and 'À son page'. The buoyant opening of the piece, with its wild clarinets in the orchestral version, becomes over-ornate and complex for the sake of complexity. Old age and death, important themes in the Ronsard cycle, were subjects which the composer was not yet ready to face. Poulenc was stretched beyond his emotional means by the song 'Le Tombeau', as it demanded that he confront the theme of death; for the occasion he adopted a Wagnerian style, most atypically for him, and even quoted what sounds like brass from Siegfried's Funeral March in Wagner's *Götterdämmerung*. Another song, 'Je n'ai plus que les os', sinks down to low notes to evoke the tomb, an example of rather conventional musical scene-painting.

Poulenc's Ronsard songs were much appreciated, especially the lament, 'Je n'ai plus que les os'. The archaic themes gave them instant classic status, but Poulenc did not recognize his own personality in these songs, feeling that they could have been written by any number of other composers. His friend Auric confirmed this feeling, advising him to write songs to poems by contemporaries like Apollinaire, Eluard and Max Jacob.

Yet Poulenc persisted in an ancient style for his next work as well. In *Chansons gaillardes*, Poulenc tried to show that obscenity could be set to mellifluous music. The songs set anonymous texts from the 1600s about wine, women, and more wine. For a polite young composer of the 1920s the *grand siècle* offered comparative sexual license, in such texts as those by Saint-Simon concerning the Roi Soleil's mistresses and the homosexual passions of his brother Monsieur. The eight songs are 'La Maîtresse volage', 'Chanson à boire', 'Madrigal', 'Invocation aux Parques', 'Couplets bachiques', 'L'Offrande', 'La Belle Jeunesse' and 'Sérénade'. Appropriately, Poulenc looked to Baroque musical forms to express these period texts: the cycle contains a sarabande ('Chanson à boire'), a sicilienne ('Sérénade') and a rash of toccatas ('La Maîtresse', 'Madrigal', 'Couplets' and 'La Belle Jeunesse').

The obscenity of these poems is limited to words like *tétons* (tits), *pucelle* (virgin) and *pucellage* (virginity). There are also risqué innuendos, as in 'L'Offrande', in which a virgin offers a candle to Cupid so that she might some day have a lover. Cupid replies, 'While you're waiting, you can use the offering.' A candle as dildo is an impish joke that might have titillated a high society gathering in the 1920s. Poulenc favoured a rapid tempo in this song, and Cupid's response was sung quietly, and the final 'Ah' quieter still. These measures were to be sung with innocence and seriousness, in order to keep the poetic feeling intact.

The title of one of the songs, 'La Belle Jeunesse', might stand for all of the *Chansons gaillardes*, which reflect a lyric and tender view of love. Obscene? Not when treated with such delicacy, charm and real art: this is Poulenc's message, aided and abetted by the great and subtle performing skill of Pierre Bernac. The songs are self-contained reflections of character with a dramatic point – almost miniature opera arias. They express exasperation at a wife's infidelity, or determination to be unfaithful to a spouse. 'Invocation aux Parques' offers the singer a chance to be uncommonly noble. Fortunately, the singer at the Paris première of *Chansons gaillardes* in May 1926 was the noble young baritone Pierre Bernac, who excelled in conveying higher feelings.

It was hard to communicate to an audience the 'scandalous double meaning' of the last song, 'Sérénade', a romantic ode to a lover's fair hand that handles Cupid's darts – 'And when this child is troubled, wipe away his tears carefully.' On another level, the troubled child is a metaphor for an erect penis, the tears semen, and the song may also be interpreted as an ode to a lover's skill as masturbator. To make this obscure double meaning more clear, Poulenc insisted that the singer link the words 'enfant est' in the phrase 'quand cet enfant est chagrin'. This pronunciation sounds odd, 'enfan-Tay', and on hearing it a French audience might sit up and notice that something was afoot and be prepared to laugh. These songs were uniquely Poulenc's: as the composer himself said, no one else could have produced this type of song, 'half-erotic and half-elegy'.

Good work poured out of Poulenc at the time, but his productivity was not without nervous strain. In September 1925 he told Stravinsky that he had gained a taste for perfection from the Russian's works, but was troubled because he lacked his 'gigantic muscles'. After attending the dress rehearsal of Stravinsky's *Oedipus Rex*, he came down with a fever and sore throat. Amid illness and inferiority complexes, Poulenc wrote *Airs chantés*, four songs to texts by a poet he despised, Jean Moréas; because Moréas was a favourite of his publisher, François Hepp, Poulenc agreed to set the texts, promising himself 'every possible sacrilege'. Moréas was a friend of Debussy, with whom he argued about Goethe's *Faust* in literary cafés. Poulenc cherished every detail about Debussy's life, but this connection was not enough to inspire him to create a major work. Even when sung by Suzanne Peignot, the *Airs chantés* sound at best like pleasant pastiches of Gluck.

Poulenc was consciously pursuing a neo-classical ideal, bearing in mind the examples of Stravinsky and Debussy. The latter's last sonatas were an attempt to revive the French classicism of Couperin's *Concerts royaux*. In his Trio for piano, oboe and bassoon which saw its first performance in 1926, Poulenc also strove for elegant symmetries and began the piece with an introduction in the French Baroque style. The work is in the traditional form of three movements, Presto, Andante and Rondo, and in an attempt to show that he was interested in musical form, Poulenc explained that the trio's first movement follows the form of a Haydn Allegro and the final Rondo, the Scherzo of Saint-Saëns's Piano Concerto No. 2.

Yet he retains a slightly ironic attitude to the Baroque tradition; the trio, for example, begins as if three card players are sadly telling each other tales of woe (Poulenc was a bridge addict). The wind instruments play a variation on the military 'Taps' – the bugle melody that mourns the military dead – while elliptical piano chords anticipate the jazz style of Duke Ellington; the three then burst into a brisk skedaddle and the conversation piece style continues, even when the oboe has lovely lyric phrases and the pianist can indulge in splashy descending chords. The trio, one of Poulenc's first mature productions, is an early model of his best qualities: balance, proportion, lyricism, humour, simplicity and clarity. His love for wind instruments shines through every measure, and while the piano dominates the three-way discourse, the bassoon and oboe never become mere accompanying instruments.

Having reached a level of professional mastery, the composer had to resolve a conflict in his personal life, that of sexual identity. As Poulenc approached thirty, social pressures came to the fore within his circle. The society painter Jacques-Émile Blanche spread a rumour that Poulenc intended to marry a daughter of Saxton Noble, Director of the Royal Academy in London, and a friend of Diaghilev. Poulenc was however concocting a scheme involving his childhood friend Raymonde Linossier: his relationship with her was certainly not physical, but he apparently had a fuzzy-edged dream of a comfy marriage of convenience, an 'open' relationship. In 1927 Poulenc bought a house in Noizay, in the Touraine countryside, and began restoring it. A year later he proposed marriage to Raymonde, not directly to the interested party but in a letter to her sister Alice. Raymonde's surviving letters to Poulenc show her to have been a tough cookie, a sharp-tongued lawyer, who abandoned legal work for a museum job. Photographs of her show a masculine face with a jutting jaw, and Poulenc may have thought his sexual identity would be settled if he married this man-like woman. He had placed Raymonde in a position of censor about his life and his music, even though she had no professional musical training. Marriage, in Poulenc's case, was as much a professional move as a personal one, as he felt that Raymonde would have a salutary influence on his work.

By 1930, when this photograph was taken at Poulenc's country home at Noizay in the Touraine region of France, the composer had decided that his life would be dedicated to wine, boys and song, though not necessarily in that order of importance.

Raymonde's disdain for homosexuals – she may have felt that Poulenc had leanings one way or another and thought her advice might influence him – was clear in her letter to Francis about Satie's funeral in Arcueil, at which 'only the chic, idle, pederastic element was represented'. Poulenc had no sexual interest in Raymonde; he told her sister Alice that immediately after the proposed marriage, when he was planning to tour America, Raymonde would be free to go to

Japan if she so wished. Raymonde was romantically involved with a Japanese man whom she had met while working as a curator at the Musée Guimet.

When Raymonde refused the offer of marriage, Poulenc was forced to realize that his ideal domestic arrangement would never be achieved. A censorious wife, always right about artistic matters, providing a domestic routine, and disapproving of pederasts, would not be present to save him from life's dangers. Francis felt abandoned and aware of the destiny his sexuality had in store for him. He suffered a nervous depression, which coincided with stirrings of love for Richard Chanlaire, a young painter whom he had met in the mid 1920s. Chanlaire, a painter of scarves and screens in his studio on the quai des Grands Augustins, was Poulenc's first great love (whereas Raymonde was his 'only deep friendship'). It was he who accompanied Poulenc on his visits to the home of Wanda Landowska outside Paris, as St-Leu-la-Forêt.

Winnaretta Singer, Princesse Edmond de Polignac, famous patron of the arts and salon hostess, as Nemesis in *Tableaux Vivants*, in 1904. Decades later she was to commission two works from Poulenc.

Poulenc had met Landowska in 1923 at the salon of Winnaretta Singer, the Princesse Edmond de Polignac – one of the most important musical patrons of her time, who commissioned works like Stravinsky's *Renard* and Satie's *Socrate*. A stout lesbian who in old age resembled George Washington, Winnaretta, heiress to the Singer sewing machine fortune, had married the homosexual Prince Edmond de Polignac. Their *ménage* may have given Poulenc his idea of a marriage of covenience with Raymonde. At the Polignac salon, Landowska's performance of the harpsichord part of Falla's *El retablo de maese Pedro* helped revive the harpsichord as a contemporary musical instrument after centuries of neglect. Modern revival of the harpsichord owed much to the Frenchman Louis Diémer (1843–1919) and later to Arnold Dolmetsch, but Landowska's combination of virtuoso aplomb and ardent personality were also decisive. Her slamming, crashing gusto and dynamism in playing Bach, Rameau, Handel and Mozart entranced Poulenc, who studied the records she made in 1923 and 1926.

The ebullient Landowska asked Poulenc to write a concerto for her. Only after visiting her at St-Leu-la-Forêt in 1926 did Poulenc have some ideas for what became the *Concert champêtre*. Unlike the austere concerto by Falla, Poulenc's was a homage to Landowska's way of vivifying old music. Thanks to her, Poulenc saw the harpsichord as

So brilliant and vibrant did Landowska's playing remain into old age that her death aged eighty shocked Poulenc, who felt he had been robbed prematurely of a great friend and irreplaceable counsellor.

carnal fun, not only as a thing of the past. Landowska insisted that the composer visit her several times to go over the work note by note, and the two rewrote much of the harpsichord part and the orchestration.

Poulenc delighted in Landowska's vibrant personality, and he could not have had a more benevolent fairy godmother presiding over his relationship with Chanlaire. Yet she ruled musical matters with an iron hand, and hurried Francis along with his first concerto: 'My God! My God! Whatever shall I do? Why are you so late?' Later, Poulenc enjoyed surprising his guests at Noizay with an impromptu drag act, descending among them dressed as Wanda Landowska, 'sensible' shoes, wig and all, and mimicking the Landowska accent.

With Chanlaire's presence inspiring him, Poulenc soon finished the *Concert champêtre*. He sent Richard a copy of the finished concerto, inscribed:

You have changed my life, you are the sunshine of my thirty years, a reason for living and working ... May this concerto always remind you of the sweet evenings at St-Leu, the brilliant and so kind Wanda, the orchestra rehearsals at Pleyel's, in short the real source of our admirable tenderness.

The emotional jolts of losing his design for living with Raymonde, and finding Chanlaire, took their toll on Poulenc. He told friends that life had broken him to the point at which he had lost his sense of identity. Poulenc made a thorough job of 'coming out', telling his friends about his love for Chanlaire. He had to revise all his friendships rapidly, given the new developments, and he suffered some bitter disappointments. Poulenc was clearly well informed about homosexuality from his time in Monte Carlo with the Diaghilev troupe – yet only now was he obliged to come to terms with the meaning of an openly gay identity.

Despite these turbulent conflicts, *Concert champêtre* is a delight, and remains one of Poulenc's most popular works. He also wrote a piano version of the *Concert*, which is never performed today, although Poulenc himself presented it in concerts. The work's large chamber orchestra, with twenty-eight string players, is considerably more dense than that of Falla in his Harpsichord Concerto or in *El retablo*. In order for the solo instrument to be heard, the special

'Landowska' model harpsichord that keyboard manufacturers Pleyel built for her should be used. A piano, or fortepiano, is closer to the built-up 'Landowska' Pleyel than an historically accurate harpsichord.

Concert champêtre is in three movements: Allegro molto, Andante and Finale (Presto). The work alternates orchestral playing with harpsichord solo passages, and its momentum never slackened when left in Landowska's hands. Inspired by the performer's energy, the first movement of the *Concert* has themes that evoke an army, and the hunt. There is a Russian lyric sweep to this movement, with airily dancing brass. Quieter moments require the harpsichord to be strummed as a harp. These effects, with a whiff of orientalia, are interrupted by gay, rapid and rhythmically marked passages that form the basis of the work. The second movement's use of the harpsichord in a *concertante* role (where a solo instrument is highlighted against an orchestral accompaniment) is ill-suited for the instrument, as Poulenc's writing required a smooth legato line which only a piano can achieve, a harpsichord making comparatively choppy sounds. The 'hunting' horns at the end of the second movement are a bow to early German Romanticism, as exemplified in the music of Poulenc's beloved Weber. The harpsichord's presence in the middle of this section is typical of Poulenc's joy in contrasting incongruous musical ideas. The final movement is marked *très gai*, but the whole work may be described this way. Landowska had the right idea when she said that she 'adored' the *Concert champêtre* because playing it made her 'insouciant and gay!' Poulenc's music allowed his friend Wanda to present herself in different guises, much as Poulenc liked to dress up as her to amuse his friends. In *Concert champêtre* the soloist dons various national musical garbs – Slavic, German, French – and sloughs them off just as quickly. The stylistic pluralism is a result of Poulenc's all-accepting *gourmandise*.

Poulenc considered that another work from the same time also belonged 'only' to Richard Chanlaire; this was the ballet *Aubade*, for piano and an ensemble of eighteen instruments. Commissioned by his friends Marie-Laure and Charles de Noailles, *Aubade* had its première in their home at the place des États-Unis in Paris's sixteenth arrondissement. *Aubade* is divided into eight musical movements: Toccata, Récitatif, Rondeau, Presto, Récitatif, Andante, Allegro féroce

Musical patron and salon hostess Marie-Laure de Noailles (1902–1970) is shown here with the composer Igor Markevich, while a solo cello work is played. Marie-Laure and Igor had a brief love affair, which Poulenc adored gossiping about to friends.

and Conclusion (Adagio). *Aubade* is usually seen as a piano concerto, but its hybrid structure does not give a convincing impression of strict concerto form. Instead, it is closer in form to the alternating movements of Rameau's opéra-ballets in the *galant* style.

Although *Aubade*'s musical organization seems fortuitous, in fact Poulenc devoted considerable thought to the way in which different themes were to blend. Among the sources for its themes are Stravinsky's *Le Sacre du printemps* and *Petrouchka*, as well as the piano music of Mozart. Poulenc added melodies that he had written previously for minor piano works, a *Sérénade* from *Trois Pièces* and a

Première Nocturne. These two melodies recur throughout *Aubade*, and create a certain unity in tying together the various strands of the work. In its percussive, rhythmic moments, *Aubade* strives for a Stravinskian ideal, whereas when the work evokes lyrical calm, the model is Mozart. The ballet includes brass fanfares and gracious eighteenth-century rondos, and at the score's most lyric moments, the piano is reduced to a role of mere accompaniment, earth-bound with percussive Lisztian virtuosity.

The first listeners to *Aubade* were surpised to find that the work evoked tears, instead of just charming them. The composer described the work as 'amphibious', with the protagonist's role shared between the woman dancer onstage and himself as pianist in the orchestra pit. *Aubade* tells of Diana the Huntress, 'burning with a love that consumes her purity'. She awakens at dawn in the forest of Fontainebleau and is dressed by her women friends. Condemned to chastity, and in despair over an impure love, she dances a variation, clasping to her breast a bow that her friends have given her; suddenly she throws away the bow and flees into the woods. The sequence of tableaux was inspired, Poulenc said, by paintings from the École de Fontainebleau.

The usually self-critical composer may have over-rated *Aubade* on account of its extra-musical associations – Poulenc, like Diana, was in a panic about a love perceived as impure. Diana's bow, like Cupid's candle in the *Chansons gaillardes*, is a symbol at once noble and phallic. Diana, condemned to eternal chastity, broke loose from her bonds; Poulenc, his path blocked to a normal lifestyle, was swept into a relationship with Chanlaire which despite his joy, he saw as impure. Sex and impurity remained synonymous for Poulenc. Like Diana, Poulenc 'disappeared into the forest' of an uncertain future. He told Ernest Ansermet before the first public performance of *Aubade* in December 1929, in Paris, that the work was a kind of tragedy. The work's portentous air sits poorly, as if in being tragic and earnest about his personal situation, Poulenc lost all perspective.

The choreographer for the Paris production, George Balanchine, ignored the plot that Poulenc had for the dance and instead introduced a handsome, muscled male dancer to portray Actéon in a *pas de deux* with Diana. The composer sputtered that his *Aubade* was a 'women's ballet', where no man should appear, but Balanchine had his way.

Stage design of Poulenc's ballet *Aubade* (1928) by Jean-Michel Frank, best known as an interior decorator. He redid the town house owned by Marie-Laure de Noailles, located at the place des États-Unis in Paris.

Opposite, a wildly humorous poet, weakly Romantic painter and martyr of the Holocaust, Max Jacob (1876–1944) provided a model for Poulenc in his unbridled sex life.

Just when Poulenc seemed to recover from his crisis, and had set to work on new projects, Raymonde Linossier died suddenly of an intestinal occlusion on 30 January 1930. Poulenc asked Raymonde's sister to bury her with the manuscript of *Les Biches* in her hands, as the work 'belongs to her'. This was done, and Poulenc added, 'All my youth departs with her, all that part of my life that belonged only to her. I sob, thinking of Monte Carlo. I am now twenty years older.' He never recovered from the loss of Raymonde as a cherished friend, and a moral and musical guide. He kept a photograph of her by his bedside when travelling, and carried her cigarette case as a talisman. Decades later, he would speak about Raymonde on important anniversaries, or in terms of his early works. Despite replacing her physical presence with more intimate relationships with men and women, he was never to find someone to accompany him who he so strongly admired. He kept in mind her attitudes and opinions – even those on homosexuality, even if they did not always alter his behaviour.

In her memory he wrote a song of formal nobility, 'Epitaphe', after a poem by Malherbe. Poulenc visualized buildings in a classical Louis XIII style while writing 'Epitaphe', in order that these images in his mind's eye might influence the melodic line. Henceforth death would be an obsession in the composer's life and and works. His mourning was expressed in a new work, one of Poulenc's greatest, *Le Bal masqué*. The 'profane cantata', set to poems by Max Jacob from the collection *Laboratoire central*, concerns the joys and terrors of French daily life. Jacob's texts, like those of Eugène Ionesco in a later generation, revealed the terrifying abyss of daily routine, of danger hidden behind banal phrases. With the atmosphere of *Le Bal masqué* as wildly comic and popular as the Cirque Medrano (a down-market fun-fair circus), it was a highly subversive work, in undermining what is generally accepted as humdrum daily reality, to reveal a monstrous underbelly, which retains its power to shock.

To have such an extreme view of the linguistic and musical norm, it helps to exist outside conventions. Max Jacob was Jewish and gay; he converted to Catholicism after Jesus Christ appeared to him in a cinema, and he wrote love poems to the Christ of a startling physical intimacy. Jacob had a promiscuous sex life, and his lovers may have included the starving teenage painter, Pablo Picasso (in spite of denials

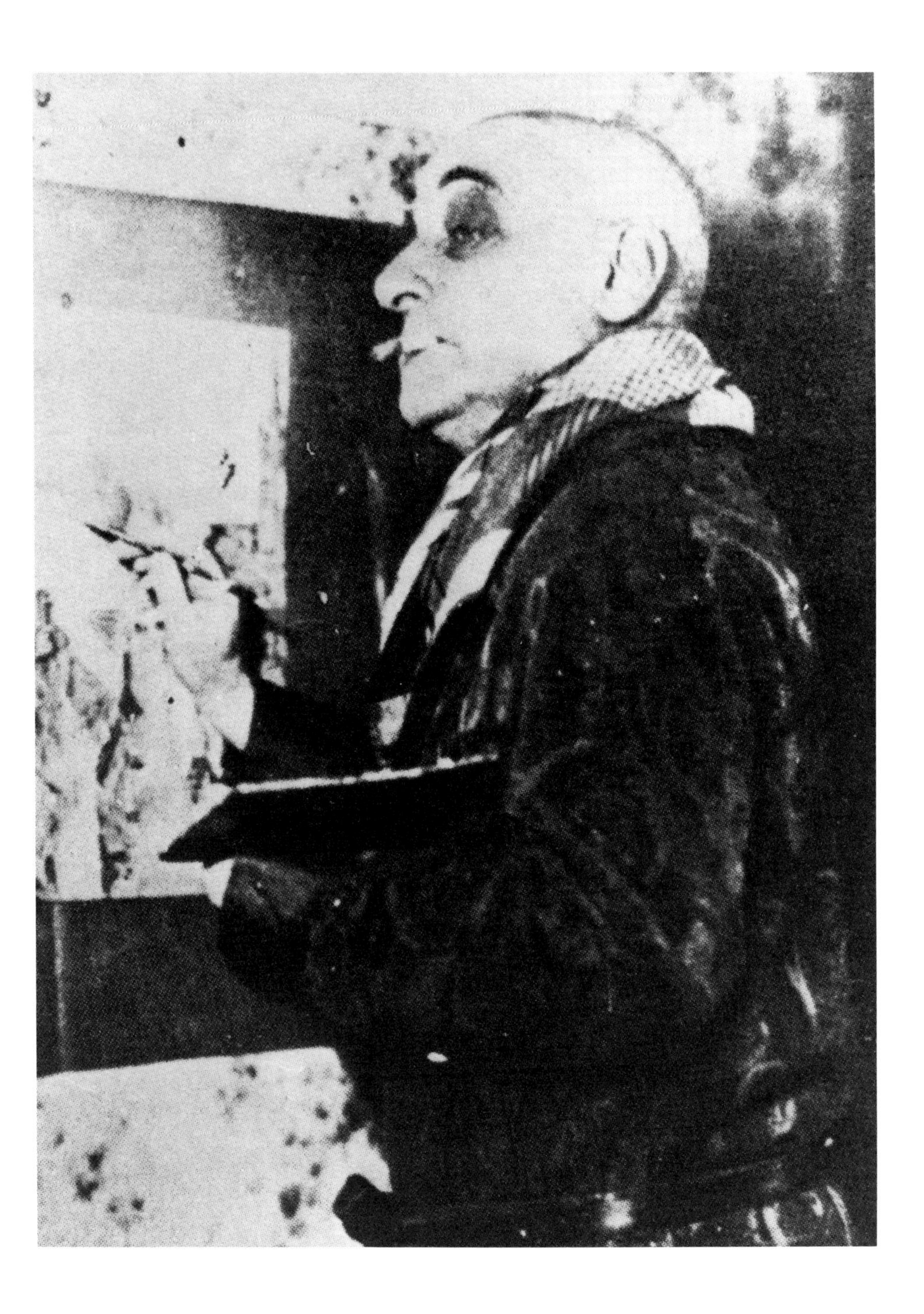

from some Picasso biographers). He became celibate in later years, retiring to a small village outside Orléans. After the German Occupation began in 1940, Jacob, like all French Jews, was obliged to wear a yellow star. His sister and brother were deported from France to Auschwitz, where they perished, and Jacob died at the French concentration camp of Drancy, in 1944, on his way to Auschwitz. Jacob's poems have been called expressions of sublimated horror over the carnage of World War I.

Le Bal masqué is the French version of the title of Verdi's opera *Un ballo in maschera,* in which brisk dance music at a ball ends in bloody tragedy, with witches and a transvestite page in the background. Poulenc produced a comparably bizarre melodrama in his 'profane cantata'. For all its delirium, it is neatly structured in six orderly sections: 'Préambule et air de bravoure', 'Intermède', 'Malvina', 'Bagatelle', 'La Dame aveugle' and 'Finale'.

Le Bal masqué begins with a whip-crack and a tawdry circus tune – the clowns enter in the spirit of Milhaud's *Le Boeuf sur le toit.* A good-time celebration is promised by the music but the text is grotesque: 'Madame la Dauphine will not see the good film they forced out of her [literally, that they made by pulling the snot from her nose] for they've laid her in the earth with her first-born, in the earth and in Nanterre where she is buried.' To give the listener a résumé in English is insufficient because Jacob's lines depend on the sound of the language: 'Car on l'a menée en terre … avec son premier né … en terre et à Nanterre … où elle est enterrée.' The mention of the banal administrative suburb of Nanterre strikes the French ear comically. Poulenc's setting of 'Madame la Dauphine-fine-fine-fine' reeks of the nursery and the music hall. An instrumental interlude, 'Intermède', between the first and second poems, allowed some breathing space from the appalling visions conjured up by the text. The potency of cheap music hovers over the second poem, the subject of which is 'Mademoiselle Malvina, agrégée ès lettres et chargée de cours', which is to say that she has a diploma in letters and a low-level academic post. She died because of love 'or let's say, diabetes'. Mademoiselle Malvina's song begins with a speedy introduction in the vein of the popular violent theatre, the Grand Guignol: 'Here's something I hope will frighten you,' followed by sinister 'mooch' music. Whips, digestive noises from wind instruments and a police whistle are topped by a Bagatelle for solo violin that evokes the diabolically gifted fiddler, Paganini, (considered by some nineteenth-century audiences to be the devil in person).

Poulenc saved the most horrid visions for later: 'The fat blind lady whose eyes bleed' ends with a passage, more spoken than sung, that shares the metaphysical horror of Berg's *Wozzeck*. At the start of the 'dame aveugle' poem the piano recalls the clock-ticking motif in the scene of Godunov's madness and death from Mussorgsky's opera *Boris Godunov*. In imagining the fat blind lady Poulenc thought of a married couple, on the île de la Beauté in Nogent-sur-Marne, around 1912. A fat rich lady used to sit on her porch with her husband, who resembled Landru, the French mass murderer portrayed in Charlie Chaplin's film *Monsieur Verdoux*. Recalling this couple was enough to inspire horror in Poulenc – to him they were emblematic of the worst that heterosexuality had to offer. The singer's falsetto cries of 'son nid!' at the end of the work could evoke either madness or transsexuality, and the frequent repetition of phrases adds to the atmosphere of obsessive mania. The words are devastating: 'In this house, everything smells of dead goatskin.' *Le Bal masqué* is an expression of the all-pervasive smell of death which Poulenc lived through following the loss of Raymonde. The sporty finale is irresistibly high-spirited, authentic popular music in its inventive orchestration.

Morbid tragedy amid circus clowning, then, is the tone of the work. Poulenc's cantata told the French: 'I am monstrous and so are you.' The grotesqueness of the work may have been slightly influenced by his patron, Marie-Laure de Noailles, who looked like a satiric portrait of royalty by Francisco de Goya. (Cecil Beaton described Marie-Laure as 'that living Daumier' while Nancy Mitford exclaimed that she 'must be seen, once!') Gilbert-Moryn, the baritone who sang in the first performance, approached *Le Bal masqué* at Poulenc's request with the same seriousness with which he sang the role of Scarpia in Puccini's *Tosca*; and indeed, the narrator in *Le Bal masqué*, like Scarpia, is in a towering sexual rage throughout. Although the lighter baritone Pierre Bernac would record this cycle, it was written for a heroic voice. *Le Bal masqué* may also be performed by a mezzo-soprano, but unfortunately it never is.

Marie-Laure de Noailles is here charitably photographed by Man Ray in his best fashion-magazine style, her equine nose de-emphasized in a full-face portrait.

One cannot long tread the line between tragicomedy and insanity represented by *Le Bal masqué*, and Poulenc reasserted the pleasure principle in other works from this time. In 1931 he set *Trois Poèmes de Louise Lalanne* and *Quatre Poèmes de Guillaume Apollinaire* which are in his best joyous vein. Louise Lalanne was a pen name for both Apollinaire and his lover Marie Laurencin. The three Lalanne songs set by Poulenc, two of which were written by Laurencin and which she disliked, are 'Le Présent', 'Chanson' and 'Hier'. According to the composer, his 'Le Présent' was inspired by Chopin's Funeral March sonata; 'Chanson' is in the same wild fairground style of *Cocardes*; 'Hier', however, is rather more musically subtle, and while writing it, Poulenc thought continually of the popular singer Yvonne Printemps and of an interior painted by Édouard Vuillard. Printemps and Vuillard may have influenced the song's clarity and simplicity (the piano part follows the vocal line almost exactly). The piano has the final, meditative word in the postlude, as it will later in *Tel Jour, telle nuit*.

The *Quatres Poèmes* are 'L'Anguille', 'Carte postale', 'Avant Le Cinéma', and '1904', all attractive melodies of excited young love. 'L'Anguille' is a *valse-musette* which seems forever ready to head off-key. The pianist was instructed by Poulenc to play in a very dry and punctuated fashion, with absolutely no pedal, rarely demanded by the composer: clearly Poulenc did not want interpreters to overdo the fun inherent in these popular songs. 'Carte postale' is a love song which Poulenc wished to be as intimate as a painting by Bonnard: again he was strict with performers, telling the pianist to play 'without nuances and strictly in the same time, moderate without dragging'. Discipline was a key to these songs, despite their open-hearted charm. 'Avant Le Cinéma' is more outwardly ironic than the other songs in the group, whereas in '1904', Poulenc once again cautioned restraint: 'do not underline exaggeratedly the erotic side; what is written suffices already.'

A sense of measure was an important element of Poulenc's art, but in life he was self-indulgent, haunted by the need not for necessities, but for luxuries. He liked to eat, drink and dress well, and loved to travel. In being coddled in ritzy hotels he could descend to an elegant lobby if he liked, to meet nice people. Poulenc had decorating crazes, like putting expensive bindings on thousands of books in his library at Noizay, even on the pocket scores. When his expenses exceeded his revenues, he feared having to sell his Touraine home and live by giving piano lessons. His letters on the subject have the air of a paranoid rich lady who fears thieves. Sergey Prokofiev, a friend and bridge partner, joked with heavy Russian irony that Poulenc should consider entering a bridge contest sponsored by *Judge Magazine*, a New York weekly, adding that the prize of 25,000 dollars paid better than commissions for compositions.

Poulenc attempted film projects with the tragic *chanteuse* Damia and the writer Colette, neither of which came to fruition. Finally he grovelled to his friends, the singer Jeanne, Comtesse Charles de Polignac, a member of Nadia Boulanger's madrigal group, and her sister-in-law Marie-Blanche de Polignac, also an accomplished singer. Both women then influenced their aunt by marriage, Winnaretta Singer, the Princesse de Polignac, to commission a work from Poulenc, which became the Concerto for Two Pianos. Poulenc had known the Princesse for many years, but she was not in a rush to commission anything from him. Once admitted to her circle of composers who were asked to create masterpieces on command, Poulenc was happy to hear the Princesse relate entertaining anecdotes; she told him that when she had invited Chabrier to perform his opera *Gwendoline* in her salon in 1888, Chabrier had passed Winnaretta the asparagus at dinner, saying, 'Try that, Madame, but it makes for an infamous urine.'

Opposite, the formidable Nadia Boulanger was a key figure in French musical education for more than half a century. A fervent supporter of Stravinsky, Boulanger offered counsel, constructive criticism and praise to Poulenc as well.

Poulenc tried to capture the joyous conviviality of the Princesse's salon in his new work. To prepare his task, Poulenc played through concertos by Mozart, Liszt, Ravel, and a piano work by Igor Markevich, *Partita.* Markevich, about ten years younger than Poulenc, was an emaciated, talented Russian composer and conductor who met Poulenc in 1928, at the time when he was filling the role of Diaghilev's last passion.

Poulenc's Concerto for Two Pianos is in three movements – Allegro ma non troppo, Larghetto and Finale: Allegro molto. Apparently in classical sonata form, the Concerto for Two Pianos was not really in the strict formal tradition based on classical models, it was more in the nature of a 'fantasie'. In this Poulenc had been greatly influenced by the two piano concertos by Ravel, in the form of fantasies: the Piano Concerto in G, which had its première in January 1932 at Paris's Salle Pleyel, and the *Concerto pour la main gauche*, from the following year. Poulenc found Ravel's new works 'marvellous' and gave an informal performance of the Concerto inG with Jacques Février at the home of Marie-Blanche de Polignac.

With the example given by Ravel, Poulenc permitted himself all liberties: although the first movement of the Concerto for Two Pianos is formally speaking divided into an introduction, development, and coda, digressions and surprises almost hide the classical structure.

Poulenc takes the listener on a silent-film adventure, in which a symphonic storm is whipped up while the two pianists pluckily continue playing. As a further splash of exotica at the end of the first movement, Poulenc added a bizarre tinkly passage, which he said was inspired by Balinese gamelan music which he had heard at the 1931 Colonial Exhibition at the Palais de Chaillot. Among other composers influenced by visits to the same gamelan concerts were Igor Markevich and Olivier Messiaen. One can understand why some critics felt that Poulenc had an everything-but-the-kitchen-sink aesthetic.

The Concerto for Two Pianos assumed classical form only to stretch it almost beyond recognition: the guiding rule was not tradition, but laughter and an appetite for sensual experience. There is gratification for the pianist in rapid climaxes and rhythmic pounding. The exchange between the two players of four notes, struck at the beginning of the work, is the sort of climax which Beethoven placed at the end of his Fourth Piano Concerto. The composer interwove this dynamic music with string pizzicatos that Brahms reserved for the end of the first movement of his Double Concerto for violin and cello. Poulenc did not make the audience wait for these winning effects, but served them up right away. The second movement begins with a close replica of a Mozart *andante*, made a trifle more precious than Wolfgang Amadeus would have written it. In contrast, the third movement seems to have been influenced by George Gershwin. The Concerto for Two Pianos, in its first movement, contains catchy jungle-boogie drums that hearkened back to Poulenc's brief early flirtation with African music in *Rapsodie nègre.*

For Poulenc, music meant fellowship and collaboration, accompaniment in every sense of the term. His 1918 Sonata for piano duet suggested a single four-handed identity, but the Concerto for Two Pianos, and the later Sonata for two pianos, could be described as conversations between two separate entities. Playful communication and one-upmanship can be sensed in the two-piano concerto, a work which gives one an idea of a humorous evening spent in the company of Poulenc. 'The rudest words, and conversational subjects, did not frighten him at all,' was Bernac's comment on Poulenc's private chatter.

Musical styles of other composers are often quoted: some rhythms recall Stravinsky and sentimental melodies, Rachmaninov; there are also folkloric castanets out of Falla's *Nights in the Gardens of Spain.* The American composer Elliott Carter, writing in *Modern Music* in January 1938, called the concerto 'a pastiche of music ranging from Scarlatti, Mozart, Schumann, Chabrier, to Stravinsky and popular songs.' Yet he also found it convincing 'because of its great verve, which, with Poulenc's remarkable sensitivity to harmonic and orchestral sonorities, ends by captivating the most stubborn listener.'

At the Venice première in 1932, Poulenc and Février performed the Concerto for Two Pianos with the La Scala orchestra, then run by Arturo Toscanini. Although Toscanini did not conduct that night, Poulenc was impressed by the quality of the musicians, calling the violins 'seraphic', the clarinets 'amorous' and oboes 'sweet and gay: Admirable!!!' Toscanini evoked from his players a combination of virtuosity and emotion that was Poulenc's instrumental ideal and which he realized in such works as the Sextet. The admiration was not reciprocal – Toscanini never conducted anything by Poulenc.

The early 1930s were years of aborted projects, such as a first version of the Sextet which would be heavily revised in 1939. Poulenc composed the stage music to Jean Giraudoux's play *Intermezzo,* directed by Louis Jouvet, and a large group of second-rate piano works were produced to please his music publishers, who found them easy to sell to amateurs. These piano pieces are relaxed and fun-loving, but of scant musical interest. Poulenc dismissed them entirely, and to take them more seriously than the composer did would be to trivialize his true achievements.

In 1934 he wrote the delightfully characterful *Quatre Chansons pour enfants* in which the view of childhood is somewhere between Hillaire Belloc's *Ruthless Rhymes* and Rossini's self-indulgent *Sins of My Old Age.* Today they tend to be sung by adult performers, but these songs might well be sung by children, as the composer intended. The first song of the four is the popular 'Nous voulons une petite soeur', in which the children's manic chorus as they pressurize their parents to produce a sister is close to the surrealist urgings to procreate in *Les Mamelles de Tirésias,* written a decade later. In its listing of the gifts the children want, 'Nous voulons une petite soeur' prefigures the greedy joys of *L'Histoire de Babar*. 'La Tragique Histoire du petit René', the second song, is about a boy who picks his nose; and the final song, 'Monsieur Sans Souci', is a parodic self-portrait like Edward Lear's 'How pleasant to know Mr. Lear'.

The time for laughter would soon be over. Economic crises would shortly be overwhelmed by new, wider-ranging difficulties that challenged the composer's world.

4

Approaching War 1936–9

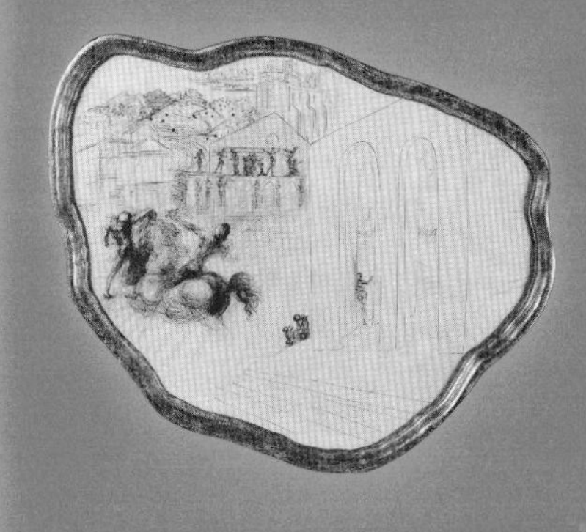

In this surrealist artwork by Salvador Dalí, commissioned by the collector and poetaster Edward James, futile combats rage. The late 1930s and 40s would be a time of constant battles, and even the insular, self-absorbed Poulenc would be affected.

I don't like this epoch, where one feels so rarely free. But I love a few people in this world … At least if I had a faith, even a negative one, that would be something. But I haven't any at all. Of course we are in an epoch where good humour alone hardly suffices for arranging matters.

Francis Poulenc, *Correspondence*

Approaching War 1936–9

By the mid 1930s economic crises and military build-ups were so evident that even a non-politicial composer would have noticed them. Fascist movements rapidly advanced in Germany and Italy. Poulenc was not involved in the anti-fascist struggle, and he wrote to his friend Henri Sauguet in October 1934, 'God knows that I'm not a diehard nationalist and that German-French reconciliations (!!!) are far from displeasing to me.' (This was no doubt a joke about a boyfriend of Poulenc or Sauguet's at the time.)

Poulenc's problem was a lack of money for luxuries; he declared 1936 a hateful year. The socialist Front Populaire led by Léon Blum did not impede the fascist advance. The Front populaire improved workers' lives (with the *congé payé*, paid holiday), but wealthy composers gained little from the movement. Poulenc abhorred French politics, right and left wing alike, saying that just because he 'vomited' the right wing did not mean that he had to kiss 'la Léon' on the mouth. Poulenc may also have been irked that in 1936 a Front populaire theatre, while ignoring him, had commissioned music from composers such as Auric, Honegger, Milhaud, Koechlin, Ibert, and Roussel: Poulenc went to the eventual show, entitled *Quatorze Juillet*, and declared that apart from what Milhaud and Auric had written, 'It's shit.' Poulenc's problems with 'the ugliness and sadness of current life, both public and private' were partly due to relationship troubles. His affair with Richard Chanlaire had fizzled out. In 1931 he inscribed the manuscript of *Aubade* to Chanlaire, 'tenderly and sadly, Francis'. He replaced Chanlaire with a handsome young bisexual chauffeur from Noizay, Raymond Destouches. As muse, Raymond would inspire Poulenc to write *Les Mamelles de Tirésias* and the choral work *Figure humaine*. But despite the coincidence of names, Raymond did not replace the late Raymonde Linossier.

As Europe headed toward a new world war, Francis spent most of his time at his country house in La Touraine, at Noizay. Busily composing, Poulenc said, 'At Noizay I have become a fat, slightly debauched monk who boasts a new and excellent cook.' At other times he complained about living in a prison of work and like all monks, was prone to *accidie*: 'I have to live through periods like the present when I despise myself and my work all day long.' Travel offered no relief from the general *malaise*. He went on tour as accompanist to the Polish soprano Maria Modrakowska, but did not relish the exotic locations. Visiting Tunisia and Algeria for concerts, he commented to friends that he felt old. Handsome soldiers there were plentiful, but he was not going to put himself at risk by pursuing them, as the composer Reynaldo Hahn did. Poulenc felt at home only in Paris or at work in the countryside, apart from a few European luxury hotels, and later, a welcoming USA.

In 1931 Poulenc set *Cinq Poèmes de Max Jacob*, portraits of Breton peasant life, consisting of 'Chanson', 'Cimitière', 'La Petite Servante', 'Berceuse', and 'Souric et Mouric'. Max Jacob artfully played with the common speech of the people, and Poulenc indulged in the kind of folklore found in Mussorgsky's song cycle *The Nursery*. 'La Petite Servante' is a speedy prayer with the neurotic intensity later echoed by Blanche's music in *Dialogues des Carmélites*. A comic waltz, 'Berceuse', was set to rude Breton language which described a list of physical discomforts to be avoided ('Deliver us from pimples … colics and diarrhoeas'); this was typical of Poulenc, a professional hypochondriac. 'Souric et Mouric' tells of a white rat and a black mouse; its setting of the words,'voici la nuit qui vient' communicates real disquiet, sung with an ominous advancing feeling, as if we are helpless to prevent the coming of darkness. As an indication of Poulenc's often abstruse thought-patterns while writing, during which he united incongruous thoughts, images and memories to create a work, he said that he always thought of his beloved wire-haired terrier Mickey, who sat under the piano as he composed, as well as a childhood friend, Eve Curie, daughter of the physicist Marie Curie.

Another group of melodies at the same time also investigated local colour and tragic emotions: *Huit Chansons polonaises* were arranged from folk melodies in 1934 for Maria Modrakowska. In Paris to study with Nadia Boulanger and Claire Croiza, Modrakowska was a writer, pianist, botanist, and chemist. Poulenc arranged war songs for her, on

MODERNE

The left-wing French political movement Le Front Populaire was headed by Léon Blum, a Jew hated by anti-Semitic nationalists but also by Poulenc, who called him 'La Léon', referring to the rumour in Paris's gay community that Blum, shown here on a poster in a 1938 Paris demonstration, was homosexual.

the theme of anxiety about death. The melodies originated in the 1831 Polish insurrection, during which people sang to boost their courage: 'If death takes you, we shall perish together ... Today we run to battle, O splendid death ... the cannon and death call me.' In writing this folkloric work Poulenc took his cue from Béla Bartók's dedicated research into folk music of Hungary and Romania. He searched for strength, and found it in his Polish women friends like Modrakowska and Landowska. To each of them he dedicated a *chanson polonaise*. Both the Max Jacob and the Polish settings used folk or peasant music in the addressing of the question of death and how to bear it. Montaigne called philosophy the art of learning how to die; Poulenc made music fill this role.

In 1936 Poulenc reached a turning point that has been misinterpreted by many. A myth exists that Poulenc was a devil-may-care member of Les Six, creating only light-hearted works; then, as one account has it, his 'dear friend' the composer Pierre-Octave Ferroud was killed in an accident, after which Poulenc wrote the simple, pious choral work *Litanies à la Vierge noire*. This commonly recounted story, however, is far from the facts. Ferroud was in fact a rival, not a friend, and he was not liked by the Poulenc crowd. He died spectacularly and violently on 17 August 1936, beheaded in a car accident. The grotesqueness of his rival's death, and its sudden brutality, made a lasting impression on Poulenc. Referring many times to the 'beheading' of Ferroud, Poulenc may have been obscurely influenced by the event later in the guillotine finale of *Dialogues des Carmélites*.

Poulenc had heard the news about Ferroud while on holiday in Uzerches. His hotel was not far from Rocamadour, the sanctuary of the *Vierge noire*, a statue miraculously sculpted in black wood by Saint Amadour. This statue, which depicts Mary with thick lips, heavy eyebrows, a beak-like nose and high cheekbones, bears an uncanny resemblance to the late Raymonde Linossier. Poulenc never wrote about this resemblance, but it is unlikely that someone as visually orientated as he would have missed the coincidence. On the evening of his first visit to Rocamadour, Poulenc began writing his first religious work, *Litanies*, based on pilgrims' prayers. The swift little work was intended to be sung simply, by a chorus of women or of children, 'in an almost rudimentary fashion' as a form of 'peasant devotion'. It has been bent out of shape by most performances and is almost always performed by women, although at one time children's choirs performed it regularly.

The *Litanies*, for women's choir, strings, timpani and organ are in one movement, which lasts about seven minutes. The mood changes from one of calm prayer to one that is 'perceptively more animated, fortissimo, exploding', (noted by the composer) when the text mentions the Virgin as protectress of medieval French warriors such as Roland, before receding to tranquillity once again. The hero of the *Chanson de Roland* was a figure appropriate to evoke a time when war threatened Europe, and Poulenc's work fits thematically with a group of young nationalistic composers inspired by mystical and religious inspiration – Jeune France, led by Olivier Messiaen and André Jolivet.

At the end of *Litanies*, as the chorus calms down, the organ adds rich new harmonies, absent from the sparse beginning, and the instrument has the final word in a quiet moment which decisively ends the piece. Poulenc wanted the organ in the *Litanies* to sound like Rocamadour's harmonium, without heaviness or undue emphasis, and Nadia Boulanger advised him on which organ registers to use for the discreet instrumental support of the choral voices.

The choral writing in *Litanies à la Vierge noire* was influenced by performances that Poulenc had heard in 1936 of Monteverdi's madrigals conducted by Nadia Boulanger, at the musical salon where his friend Marie-Blanche de Polignac sang soprano in these concerts. But women's choral groups often have the opportunity to sound operatic in the *Litanies* – a foreshadowing of *Dialogues des Carmélites* – cries of 'ayez pitié de nous' retain an overinsistent, irritated tone. The shrillness may have had its origin in Poulenc's lack of sure faith. He told Auric:

I don't like this era where one feels so little free ... I'd like to be able to think as you do, to have your faith ... If I had some kind of faith, even a contrary one, that would be something, but I absolutely don't.

The *Litanies* reveal a passionate, but unfulfilled desire to believe, which is the anguished source of Poulenc's religious music. By contrast, a choir of children singing the work underlines its folkloric aspects.

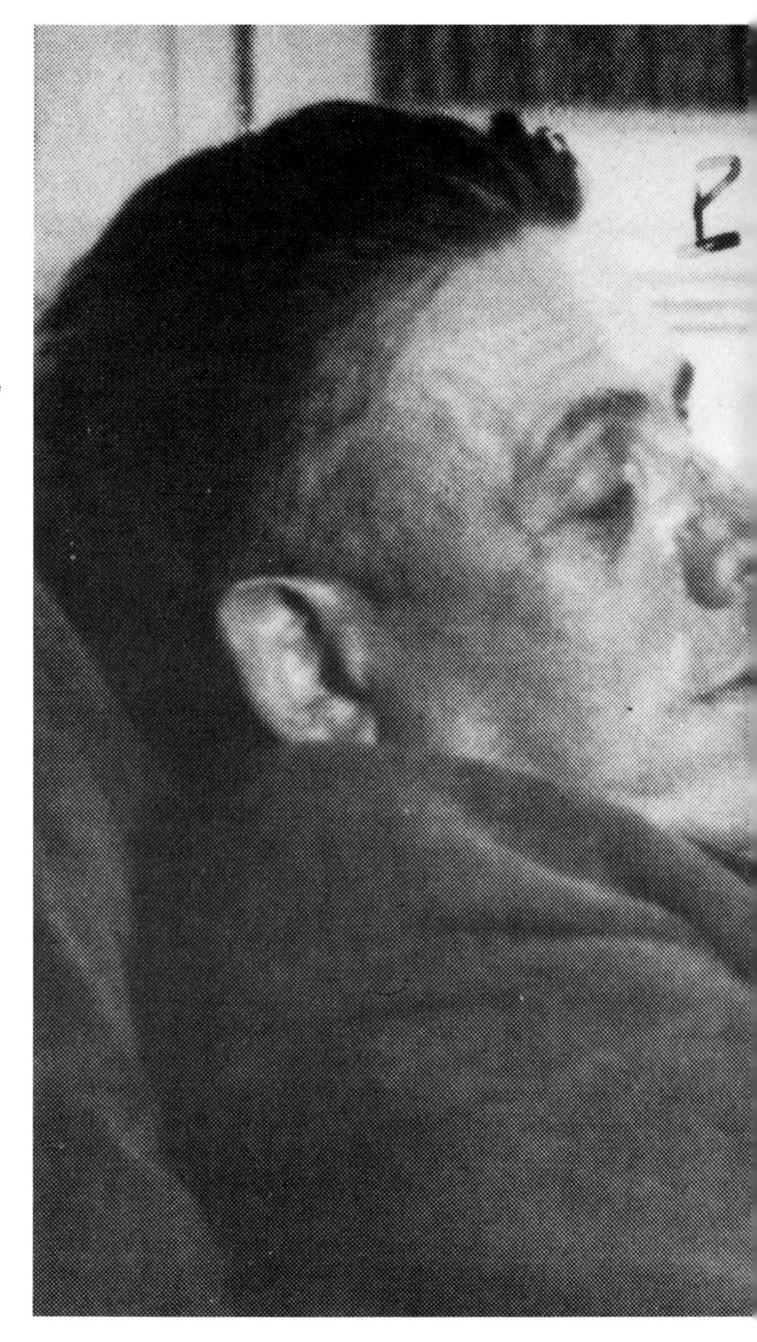

Poulenc was a confirmed dog-lover, and wrote one into a late work, his opera *La Voix humaine*. This image of utter satisfaction shows the composer with his beloved terrier Mickey, also known as 'Toutou'.

Children were a constant theme in Poulenc's life and work. Needless to say, Poulenc's interest in children was not pederastic. He valued their overwhelming energy, their freshness and often, rudeness. As a concentration of rebellious energy, children served as inspiration for Poulenc's playful works for his entire career. On a number of occasions, he dedicated works to children, and not just to flatter their parents, who might range from his friends to his music publishers. In 1936 Poulenc produced *Petites Voix*, five *a cappella* choral works for three voices easy enough to be performed by children.

The composer would soon benefit from the advice of one of his major musical authorities. In June 1934, after one of Pierre Bernac's recitals of Debussy in Paris, Poulenc expressed a desire to accompany Bernac in his own songs, as well as those of Debussy. The same summer, when Poulenc went to the Salzburg Festival as a journalist for *Le Figaro*, Bernac was hired to give a Debussy recital for an eccentric rich lady tourist, but lacked a pianist. He sent Poulenc a note, asking for his help, adding the promise: 'Good pay'. Poulenc accepted. In 1935 he began to tour with Bernac, accompanying his vocal recitals, one of the main motivations being a financial one. Poulenc had asserted, 'I prefer to play the piano rather than to write inferior and venal music,' but in 1935 he had written music for a cartoon publicity film for Nicolas wineshops, which was shown in Paris cinemas. Accompanying song recitals was certainly less venal than that.

Opposite, the baritone Pierre Bernac, here shown with Poulenc in 1937, was a much-valued counsellor for musical matters in general and vocal questions in particular. Despite a slightly quacking sound to his voice that distracted a few listeners, Bernac was a great and refined interpreter of Poulenc's works.

Poulenc had always found fine singers to interpret his songs. Gilbert Moryn, the baritone praised by Poulenc, had given the first performances of *Le Bal masqué* and the *Quatre Poèmes de Apollinaire*, but soon faded out of the picture. The soprano Maria Modrakowska, another favourite of Poulenc's, suddenly retired from singing in 1935 without any explanation. Poulenc's collaboration with Bernac proved more durable, perhaps in part because Bernac's career was limited to song recitals, and thus he had no conflicting engagements. Poulenc had ignored Bernac for eight years before their Salzburg recital together. Both men kept their distance from one another, because each had heard the rumour (untrue) that Bernac, from an upper-class French family, was pained by the rudeness of the *Chansons gaillardes*. The intervening years were formative for Bernac, and by the time he sang again with Poulenc he was a mature artist aged thirty-four. All

the composer had to do was to play the piano accompaniment to the ninety songs that he created for Bernac over twenty-five years: no energy needed to be lost in training him to perform correctly.

Poulenc wrote songs for Bernac as a person, as much as for his voice. The baritone's versatility and technical ease meant that he could intepret works written for others than himself, such as *Le Bal masqué*, for which the composer had intended a more heroic, rousing voice. But Bernac's singing was subtle, with finely honed degrees of expressivity and dynamics. Above all, he could communicate nobility, and convincing amorous involvement, both essential for the romantic texts he interpreted. Bernac possessed the typically French quality of analytical clarity and Poulenc knew that he could show every new work to Bernac, and rely on an objective, rational reaction. Poulenc admitted that Bernac was 'always right'. Utterly frank and honest with his friend, Bernac was also a polite, genteel and private man. His modest-sized voice, like his personality, seemed completely under control, and his level-headedness permitted Poulenc to play the star in their professional duo. On tour, most of the unpleasant chores, such as booking railway tickets and hotel reservations, were left to the baritone. Poulenc, who hated rehearsing, preferred to browse through the local museums. Later, Poulenc was to sum up their 25-year-long professional partnership by placing Bernac among the 'three great meetings' of his career, the others being with Landowska and the poet Paul Eluard.

His first professional contact with Eluard dated from the same time, in the mid 1930s. But Poulenc had met Eluard years before in Adrienne Monnier's bookstore: 'I had a weakness for Eluard right away, because he was the only surrealist who tolerated music. Also because all his work is a musical vibration.' In 1935 he set five of Eluard's poems for Bernac: 'Peut-il se reposer?', 'Il la prend dans ses bras', 'Plume d'eau claire', 'Rôdeuse au front de verre' and 'Amoureuses'. Until 1948 and the Apollinaire cycle *Calligrammes*, Poulenc would focus principally on Eluard's work. He later disliked the *Cinq Poèmes de Paul Eluard*, considering them inferior to the songs that he had written earlier to poems by Apollinaire and by Max Jacob, and to those he would later write to Eluard. Curiously, the problem seemed to lie more in the piano part than in Bernac's interpretation of the vocal line. In 'Amoureuses' the piano is loud, and the composer confessed he had attempted a maximum of expression with a minimum of musical means; in 'Rôdeuse au front de verre' he was reduced to repeating some Balinese-style music from the Concerto for Two Pianos. But generally the *Cinq Poèmes de Paul Eluard* suffer from an unnecessary complexity and unsteady rhythms, considering the limpid mastery that Poulenc would soon achieve, when working on other texts by the same poet. Yet in writing the *Cinq Poèmes,* Poulenc stated that he had recalled a 1932 exhibition of Matisse's illustrations of Mallarmé's poems: he had hoped to imitate the way in which Matisse, after many efforts, reduced his thought to a single, essential line. Only 'Plume d'eau clair' achieved something of this Matisse ideal; its clear harmonies and steady rhythm led Poulenc to say that although he had searched for a musical key to Eluard's poems for years, only in this song did it 'squeak in the keyhole'.

In 1936 he decided to set five poems from Eluard's new collection, *La Vie immédiate.* Poulenc first tried to write these songs to a piano accompaniment, but then decided that a piano could only weigh them down. Instead, like the *Litanies à la Vierge noire,* the work, *Sept Chansons,* revealed the influence of unaccompanied Monteverdi madrigals. Poulenc had learned from the performances of Boulanger's group the Monteverdian way of mixing voices, and techniques such as singing with the mouth closed. Most of all, Poulenc assimilated from Monteverdi's art a sense of just measure.

Poulenc went against the examples of Debussy and Ravel, who wrote *a cappella* choral works using old texts, or texts in the antique style. Poulenc chose to be resolutely modern in applying modern poetry to the ancient tradition of French polyphonic music of the Renaissance, part-songs at which composers like Janequin and Le Jeune excelled. But Poulenc also had an orchestral ideal in mind, and so wrote for a large choir. The critic Hélène Jourdan-Morhange pointed to the link between *Sept Chansons* and the instrumental style of 'conversation pieces', in which instruments seem to discuss intimate matters among themselves.

Because the five Eluard poems he chose were all sombre, he feared the work might be too static, so he added two more dynamic poems by Apollinaire, strategically placed in what finally became the choral work *Sept Chansons*: 'Blanche Neige' (Apollinaire), 'À peine défigurée' (Eluard), 'Pour Une Nuit nouvelle' (Eluard), 'Tous Les Droits' (Eluard), 'Belle et Ressemblante' (Eluard), 'Marie' (Apollinaire), and 'Luire' (Eluard).

When Poulenc asked permission to use the two poems by Apollinaire, Gaston Gallimard, the publisher who controlled the

Vous trouverez ici une nouvelle représentation

tout terriblement

Guillaume Apollinaire

Apollinaire's poignant, lovelorn melancholy moved Poulenc as a reader and composer, giving him sympathy for the poet's *Calligrammes*, whether scribbled in letters (as here, in a horse calligram) or arranged formally on the printed page.

rights, refused. Apollinaire's widow Jacqueline intervened in Poulenc's favour, but Gallimard was dead-set against Poulenc and she did not have the final say. He was not prepared to accept defeat because of what he called 'the spitefulness of the *maison Gallimard*'. Denied the Apollinaire texts he needed, Poulenc envisaged asking Max Jacob to write new verses to go along with his already-composed choral music. Finally, the work was presented in 1943, with other words cobbled to the two Apollinaire settings. Gallimard heard the work, and decided belatedly to give his permission.

At Christmas 1936 Poulenc played Bernac his setting for Jean Cocteau's *Plain-Chant*. When Bernac was not enthused by what he heard, Poulenc threw the musical manuscript into the fire; on seeing Bernac's horrified expression, Poulenc laughed and told him not to worry – there would be something better for their next scheduled recital in February.

The result, *Tel Jour, telle nuit*, was from its first performances considered a masterpiece: the critic and composer Roland-Manuel placed it alongside Schumann's *Dichterliebe* and Schubert's *Die Winterreise*. Part of the reason why *Tel Jour* achieved such instant classic status, apart from its lyrical emotion, was its strong sense of structural unity. In the tradition of French song cycles, from Berlioz's *Nuits d'été* to Fauré's *La Bonne Chanson*, context and continuity are considered as important as isolated melodic inspiration. Poulenc recognized as much, admiring the talent for structure in *La Bonne Chanson* by a composer whom otherwise he detested. For his new work, Poulenc was inspired directly by song cycles he admired: he added a piano postlude to the cycle like the one in *Dichterliebe*, 'to allow the audience to prolong the emotion'.

Carefully structuring *Tel Jour*, Poulenc compared its composition to the hanging of paintings in a museum: some of the songs were 'principal' ones, while others were transitional, or what Poulenc called 'trampoline' songs. The cyclic rhythm of the songs was carefully planned, its nine melodies varying in tone from elegiac to violent: 'Bonne Journée' (elegy); 'Une Ruine coquille vide' (elegy); 'Le Front comme un drapeau perdu' (forward-moving); 'Une Roulotte couverte en tuiles' (slow, sad); 'À Toutes Brides' (fast, violent); 'Une Herbe pauvre' (slow, sad); 'Je n'ai envie que de t'aimer' (forward-moving);

'Figure de force brûlante et farouche' (fast, violent); 'Nous avons fait la nuit' (elegy). The emotional variations were alternated in a satisfyingly symmetrical way. Although consciously planned by the composer, this artfulness sounds utterly natural and inevitable, which is part of the greatness of the music. As part of the cyclic structure, the first and last songs are in the same key of C major, and share the same tempo and a similar vocal line.

The poems Poulenc chose have strong moral and social concerns. *Tel Jour* speaks of what Eluard called 'the fine glance of people deprived of everything', crying with misery in the streets, in prisons and other surreal landscapes of misery. In the cycle, a lover is obsessed with his beloved's body as a reflection of the world around him. Poulenc recounted how he began writing the songs after a Proustian triggering of childhood memory. Searching for inspiration, Poulenc had been strolling along Paris's avenue Daumesnil in the Bastille quarter. Suddenly he saw a surrealist vision of 'a locomotive in a tree', part of the elevated railroad. This was the train he took from Paris to Nogent-sur-Marne. During his childhood Francis had marvelled at the elevated railroad at the Bastille, which blended with the trees on a second-storey level. Confronted by the surreal image, Poulenc thought of the leading surrealist lyric poet, Paul Eluard, whose poems he was trying to set and started to recite the poem 'Bonne Journée' to himself. That evening, he began to write the song cycle.

Of the last song, 'Nous avons fait la nuit', Bernac said: 'We must imagine the two lovers side by side in bed, having turned out the light, "made the night", the man "holding the hand" of the woman and "supporting her with all his force …"' That Poulenc should have so sincerely portrayed this scene is one of the surprises of art. His emergence as a composer of love songs was as surprising as when W. H. Auden published his 'Lay Your Sleeping Head, My Love,' which may be compared to 'Nous avons fait la nuit' as one of the most celebrated love lyrics of its time. Poulenc offered an affirmation of the strength of human affections and his continuing relationship with Raymond Destouches may have been one uncredited source of his new lyricism. In the song there is no sense of a homosexual creator transposing the sexes, as critics claim Marcel Proust did in replacing the image of his beloved Albert with his Albertine. Heterosexual love is profoundly expressed in *Tel Jour, telle nuit*, even in the title's symmetrical contrast between the masculine, 'le jour', and the feminine, 'la nuit'. Poulenc so identified with his poet that he achieved one of the great odes to physical love between a man and woman. It is not therefore surprising that his talent was also sufficient to create moving religious music.

Poulenc stressed that calmness was necessary to sing the poems in *Tel Jour, telle nuit*; this was also true of his Mass in G, written in 1937 for four-part *a cappella* choir. The Mass has five movements, Kyrie, Gloria, Sanctus, Benedictus and Agnus Dei; a Credo movement was conspicuously lacking. One commentator hasarded a guess that Poulenc omitted a Credo from his Mass because he was 'guided by a faith so secure that he apparently felt no need to state it outright.' One might equally assume that he left out the Credo because his faith was recent and relatively insecure, or simply that in this brief Mass, what was left out in general was as striking as what was included – there is no orchestra nor even an organ to accompany the Mass in G. Although written for men and women singers together, sopranos dominate the mass, as they did in the *Litanies à la Vierge noire*. Religious worship was in Poulenc's sonic imagination an affair for pious country women.

The opening Kyrie has strongly confrontational harmonies, which Poulenc said were meant to evoke the early days of the Church when non-baptized people were permitted to sing alongside the priests. The bareness of the unaccompanied voices represents the craggy primitiveness of religion that Poulenc cherished on pilgrimages to Rocamadour. Having begun his composing career influenced by rhythms from Africa, twenty years later, in *Litanies* and the Mass in G, Poulenc sought a new wildness in the humblest aspects of Catholic worship.

The Gloria, marked 'very animated', is a war march, part of a militant type of Catholicism which was much in vogue in the 1930s in France: the Action Française movement, led by writers like Léon Bloy and Léon Daudet, aggressively promoted the Catholic religion as part of a package with fascism, nationalism, and anti-Semitism. Although Poulenc was anything but a political activist, his Mass, charged with energy, may have reflected an aspect of popular Catholicism of the time.

The Sanctus is marked 'very much going forward and sweetly joyous'. Poulenc said that when writing this movement he imagined the heads of angels sticking out their tongues at one another in a fresco by the fifteenth-century painter Benozzo Gozzoli in Florence's Palazzo Ricardi; he called the vocal effect of the Sanctus a 'carillon of voices'. The Benedictus, 'calm but not slow' keeps the joyous and vigorous tone of the work intact; Poulenc was clearly trying to communicate his feelings of attraction towards religion and to be evangelical in the most charming way possible.

The final movement, Agnus Dei, starts with the first of those high arching soprano solos which would add so much glamour to the later works *Gloria* and *Stabat Mater*. When the choir sings, 'miserere nobis' (have pity on us), the request is a charmingly shy one, as if asking a favour of a dear friend, with an embarrassed grin. The Mass in G has become a classic with skilled choral groups, particularly in England and America. The American composer Aaron Copland reviewed a 1938 recording of the Mass in the magazine *Modern Music*: 'Eclectic as ever, charming as ever, musical as ever, this Mass is not at all severe and forbidding. *Au contraire*. It was meant to be sung in all simplicity in a sunny church in Southern France.'

Poulenc's next work was a step backward in many ways. *Sécheresses*, a cantata for mixed choir and large orchestra, was written to four poems by the surrealist art collector and poetaster Edward James. Poulenc accepted the commission not because he liked James's verse but because he wanted the money. James offered nearly twice what Winnaretta Singer would pay in 1938 for the commission of the organ concerto: 20,000 francs compared to 12,500. The project also gave Poulenc the chance to write for chorus and orchestra, which he had not done since the unsatisfactory choral interludes of *Les Biches*.

Sécheresses was divided into four movements – 'Les Sauterelles', 'Le Village abandonné', 'Le Faux Avenir', and 'Le Squelette de la mer'. The work's sombre, hard-edged sounds would find echoes in Poulenc's later production, including the *Stabat Mater* (1950), *Dialogues des Carmélites* (1957) and *Sept Répons de Ténèbres* (1961). *Sécheresses*, for all its skill, gives the impression of a composer trying to throw the entire *Treatise of Orchestration* by Berlioz at the public so as not to hear the poems that the choir is singing.

Opposite, wildly eccentric and very wealthy, the bisexual Edward James (1908–84) commissioned a number of paintings (by Dalí) and musical compositions (Poulenc's *Sécheresses*).

Poulenc himself referred to the 'flaming giraffes' style of the opening of *Sécheresses*, inspired by Salvador Dalí. Overall, there is an 'instant classic' air to this work which sits badly today. Bossy and opinionated, James offered lots of advice about the music, and Poulenc confessed shamefacedly to a friend, 'I ceded to James because he ... paid ... me for the work. I wanted him to be happy. You saw the results.' In the last movement, James had advised Poulenc to insert an orchestral passage after the words 'écoutez-moi'. Eager to please his patron, Poulenc agreed, but later deleted the passage, furious with himself for having acceded, and saying the effect was like a man saying 'Listen to me', before leaving the room only to return ten minutes later to explain himself. Expecting a neo-classical delight, the Paris public got a work of grandeur and gravity, and gave it a glacial reception. When Poulenc wanted to destroy it, Georges Auric persuaded him otherwise, feeling that one of the reasons for its failure was that he had not relied on his sense of prosody. *Sécheresses* showed how vital it was for Poulenc to have a personal connection with the poems he set.

Poulenc had decided years before that he preferred to set poems by living writers whom he knew personally, and like Schubert, he would choose some texts because he liked the person who wrote them. An uneven poem by a friend was an unfinished item which needed to be infused with music in order to make it live. By composing music, Poulenc vivified what was otherwise dormant, and thus might be seen to give concrete evidence of the friendship. This would explain why he set so many poems by the minor poet Louise de Vilmorin, an experienced seductress who wrote coy, fey verses.

She would provide poems for three cycles by Poulenc: *Trois Poèmes* (1937), *Fiançailles pour rire* (1939) and *Métamorphoses* (1943). Poulenc claimed to find in her poetry 'a sort of sensitive impertinence, libertinage, and appetite which carried on into song what I tried to express in my extreme youth with Marie Laurencin in *Les Biches*.'

Opposite, although Poulenc thought of Dalí's surrealism while composing *Séchéresses*, he found Dalí unoriginal, and had little sympathy for Gala, who ran away from her husband Paul Eluard to live with Dalí.

Loulou, as everyone called her, was to end her life as the companion of André Malraux; she had a limp, which created as much sympathy as her ethereal elegance. Some observers were more resistant to Loulou's charms than Poulenc. Evelyn Waugh met her just after World War II, and described her to Nancy Mitford as 'an Hungarian countess who pretended to be a French poet. An egocentric maniac

with the eyes of a witch. She is the Spirit of France. How I hate the French.' To which Nancy Mitford replied: 'Darling Evelyn, oh how glad I am you feel this about Lulu – I can't sit in a room with her she makes me so nervous. And vicious ... She is much more like a middle European than a French woman.'

Vilmorin's verse allowed Poulenc to return to the idyllic Monte Carlo of the 1920s when he was preparing *Les Biches* for Diaghilev. Not yet forty years old, Poulenc already had an old man's nostalgia for the past. His first effort to set her work, in *Trois Poèmes de Louise de Vilmorin*, was first performed in 1938 by the composer and Marie-Blanche de Polignac. The three songs 'Le Garçon de Liège', 'Au-delà', and 'Aux Officiers de la garde blanche' make up the group. In the first two, Poulenc tried to write a 'palpitating' piano part that communicated wild romantic desire ('Le Garçon de Liège' is meant to be played 'vertiginously fast'); the third song, in contrast, is more serious and melancholy, and its accompaniment imitates a guitar. Vilmorin often played 'Aux Officiers ...' at parties, with an overall sadness and gravity.

Louise de Vilmorin was living in Hungary with her husband when the war broke out, and Poulenc wrote his main cycle of her poems, *Fiançailles pour rire* (1939), as a way of retaining emotional closeness to his friend. Narrated by a woman singer, the cycle is Poulenc's answer to Schumann's *Frauenliebe und -leben.* A sense of intimate fondness (and sometimes hoydenish sentimentality) is common to both works. Vilmorin's attitudes towards life and chivalrous love had not developed far beyond Schumann's nineteenth-century Romanticism. *Fiançailles* contains six songs, 'La Dame d'André', 'Dans l'herbe', 'Il Vole', 'Mon Cadavre est doux comme un gant', 'Violon', and 'Fleurs'. The work is the plaint of a disillusioned society lady, and Poulenc's narrator is bitter and arch, calling her betrothal a joke. The biting tone recalls the wit of Raymonde Linossier, who had refused to take Poulenc's marriage proposal seriously a decade before. The words are ungainly, over-refined and brittle. The poet asserts, 'My corpse is soft as a glove ... and my two feet are mountains.' Poulenc told a friend that the *Fiançailles* had 'a completely different tone from the *Trois Poèmes.* It's profoundly melancholic and lyrical. The last, 'Fleurs', is a tear-jerker, or ought to jerk them, at least ...'

The poem 'Mon Cadavre est doux comme un gant' mixed erotic themes with morbidity, but Poulenc's sombre melody focuses only on death. 'Violon', written by Vilmorin in homage to the gypsy violins of Hungary, the native land of her husband, Count Palffy, was transformed into Nogent dance-hall style by Poulenc.

Poulenc had originally intended *Fiançailles* to be the woman's counterpart to *Tel Jour, telle nuit*, but he soon realized that it did not match the earlier cycle in quality. From the earliest structural sketches, Poulenc thought of song-placement in terms of varied emotional mood. He would sometimes spend years tinkering with a melody. He described how he had planned the cycle, as follows: '1. Dame d'André; 2. grave melody; 3. lively melody; 4. Mon cadavre; 5. gay melody'. At first he thought to place 'Fleurs' as the second song, but decided that it would be better at the end of the cycle, next to a song in a different key which would set it off well. Poulenc added 'Violon' to the cycle after his original plan, making six songs in total.

Fiançailles was given its première with the composer at the piano, accompanying the soprano Geneviève Touraine in May 1942 in Paris. The cycle is often performed and recorded, although Poulenc himelf considered it 'fabricated'. A song cycle for a woman is a rarity in the popular classical repertoire, and other Poulenc cycles, such as *Tel Jour, telle nuit*, adapt oddly for women's voices.

Deux Poèmes de Guillaume Apollinaire (1938) were in every sense an improvement on the Vilmorin settings. Poulenc's 'Dans Le Jardin d'Anna' from this set was the diametrical opposite of *Sécheresses*, where the music was designed to hide the poor quality of the words. Poulenc followed each detail with craftsmanship and ease, illustrating his affinity with Apollinaire's world, which he could recreate in a natural way. The poem is about love, and also contains ironic comments such as 'If I happened, unfortunately, to be German', which were especially timely in 1938. Because the song contained a long series of images, Poulenc stressed that it had to be performed in the same strict continuous tempo. 'Allons plus vite' ('Let's go faster'), the second of the 1938 Apollinaire settings, evokes a city landscape infused with melancholy and pain. The title is a reiterated command to a prostitute who is being hurried along a boulevard by a client.

In 1939 Poulenc set another Apollinaire text, 'Bleuet', as an anti-war statement. This heartfelt song about a young soldier 'who knows death better than he does life' was written at the same time as another Apollinaire setting, 'La Grenouillière', about how the pleasures of youth were past. 'La Grenouillière' is the name of an island on the Seine outside Paris, where weekend revellers danced and dined a century before, as in Renoir's famous painting, *Le Déjeuner des canotiers.* The rhythm of the song, according to Poulenc, was based on the canoes of revellers knocking into one another. He wanted to retain an emotional atmosphere of tenderness that would discourage laughter for the lines about 'women with fat chests, stupid as cabbages'.

A solitary Eluard setting, 'Ce doux petit visage' (1938), also described nostalgia for the past, while anticipating war: 'youth, which flees before life'. The limpidity of this particular song was partly due, Poulenc believed, to his Pleyel piano in Noizay, which was far softer in tone than the dry Erard piano Ravel worked on or Debussy's smooth-sounding Bechstein. Two other poems by Paul Eluard made up the cycle, *Miroirs brûlants* (1938): 'Tu vois le feu du soir' and 'Je nommerai ton front'. The first of these states, 'You see the beautiful child, when he plays, when he smiles ...' Poulenc, who longed for a family of his own, doted on the children of his friends, and felt nostalgia for the purity that children represented. (As they age, humans retain only the monstrous aspects of childhood, as in *Le Bal masqué.*) At the mention of a 'beautiful child' in 'Tu vois le feu du soir', the harmony has an air of sanctity, as it would in Poulenc's later sacred motets about Christ's nativity. Poulenc said that he admired humility in prayer and in music; he was moved by child-like vulnerability.

Poulenc stressed that in performance 'Tu vois le feu du soir' should be taken at a constant pace, as it contained a long series of successive images, as did his setting of Apollinaire's 'Dans Le Jardin d'Anna'. In the Eluard song he strove to avoid monotony in setting such a long text by composing an ever-inventive, varied piano part to an extremely simple vocal line. Poulenc agonized over the details, such as in the line 'à l'été qui la couvre de fruits', because the syllable 'té' was set to a high note, which he feared would create difficulties for singers, since 'té' is usually pronounced with the throat closed, and singers benefit

Opposite, the painter Marie Laurencin in a languid pose, as photographed by Poulenc

from open, relaxed throats to achieve notes in a high range. After consulting Bernac, however, Poulenc decided to leave the high note as it was.

From such minutiae in finely-honed miniatures, Poulenc switched to one of his largest-scaled orchestral works, the Organ Concerto. One reason behind its creation was financial: composing songs did not offer a secure income. Poulenc had begged the Princesse de Polignac for another commission and Winnaretta replied that she could only afford to pay him half the previous sum because 'thanks to Mr. Roosevelt, my musical budget is considerably reduced.' She asked Poulenc to write for a rarely used instrument, preferably her Cavaillé-Coll organ. He dated his Organ Concerto 'April–August 1938', perhaps to bring it retrospectively closer to wartime, but a first version was finished in 1936. Poulenc's Organ Concerto is loved by audiences and record companies because it reveals the full range of the instrument; it is the loudest and most hysterical of solo instruments, as the concerto amply demonstrates, but there are also quieter, small-scale, harmonium-like passages similar to some of the accompaniments in the *Litanies à la Vierge noire*.

Poulenc enjoyed attending concerts by organ virtuosos of the day, particularly those of Marcel Dupré, who reigned over the organ at St Sulpice. Maurice Duruflé, the young virtuoso who was to give the première of the work, was asked by Poulenc how to achieve 'that sort of tedious drone' that church organs often have. Poulenc was also advised on organ matters by the Polignac's musical adjutant, Nadia Boulanger, the tall and strapping 'Mademoiselle' who terrorized generations of music students. Her own organ teacher, Albert Schweitzer, along with the composer Louis Vierne, had been amongst the group of astonishingly vibrant organists in Paris at the time – these performers opened blast furnaces of emotion with each solo piece. Their recordings illustrate the kind of catharsis Poulenc expected from his Organ Concerto, which was to be an expression of unleashed anxiety and panic.

In choosing the organ as solo instrument Poulenc was returning to his traditionalist father's admiration of César Franck, head of the nineteenth-century French organ school. Yet Poulenc rejected the usual three-movement concerto format which he had used in *Concert champêtre* and the Concerto for Two Pianos. Instead he looked to the structure of *Aubade*, a series of intertwined movements in the form of a *ricercar* (a sixteenth- and seventeenth-century musical form in which themes are disguised through a number of artifices).

Poulenc, abandoning the classical format of three movements (fast–slow–fast), offered an emotional voyage in which it is difficult to find one's bearings – a reprise of certain melodies from the beginning of the work does not give it symmetry. Poulenc referred to the upcoming war as 'this horrible tornado', and the Organ Concerto is an attempt to create a tornado of beauty, a work that would be as operatic as possible without actually being an opera. The organ is a monstrous continuation of the human voice, with its infinite wind, volume, and dynamic range. The composer reflected, 'I don't see myself writing a pompous *Te Deum* for Notre Dame.' Yet the Organ

Like his friend Auric, shown here wining and dining with Dalí and the Comtesse Etienne de Beaumont, Poulenc wasted many evenings in high society, showing off to the idle rich.

Concerto had plenty of pomp and has remained Poulenc's most popular instrumental work for church performance. The work opens with a fanfare that brings to mind a Bach Fantasia. Caressing Italianate strings and rolling tambours follow, with blasts from the organ, conjuring up the terrifying open maw of death. The rapid-paced melody in the second movement hurries onwards, but to nowhere good. The stark outlook is accentuated by the obsessive repetition of limited thematic material. The Organ Concerto has been accepted by a large public as a splashy virtuoso showpiece (in the vein of Saint-Saëns's 'Organ' Symphony). Yet Poulenc's work is more complex than this, as it has a clear sense of an ongoing procession to doom.

Shortly after the concerto was finished, Winnaretta Singer left France for England where, as an American, she would be in less danger. Poulenc never saw her again, for she died in exile in 1943. Before dying, she declared, 'Faced by what seems to be the end of it all for an old lady like me, I proclaim that I always loved music, paintings, and books more than anything else, and I was right!'

After the operatic Organ Concerto, Poulenc was inspired to compose an opera. He discussed projects with Armand Lunel, a librettist for his friends Darius Milhaud and Henri Sauguet, and suggested that Lunel study the libretto of Verdi's *Otello*, 'where something really happens'. Poulenc also considered the story of Balzac's *La Fille aux yeux d'or*, which contains a lesbian theme, and Stendhal's *Abbesse de Castro* for its historical-romantic atmosphere and stage effects. Later they discussed the idea of a *Youth of Gargantua*, after Rabelais. But for the moment, sacred choral works keyed to emotions of the time came first. Having heard premières of two tragic Milhaud works, *Cantates de la paix* and *Deux Cités*, Poulenc set to work on four motets for holy week; these he wanted to be as solidly realistic as a Mantegna painting. The musical model for the *Quatre Motets pour un temps de Pénitence* (1938–9) was Tomas Luis de Victoria (1548-1611), whom Poulenc considered the 'Saint John of the Cross of music'.

The first motet, 'Timor et tremor', was composed to Latin words from the Vulgate of Psalms 54, 56 and 30: 'Fear and trembling have come upon me, and darkness has covered me over. Have pity on me,

Lord ...' The emotional tone of this movement develops from anguish to calm affirmation. The second motet, 'Vinea mea electa', inspired by a passage from the book of Isaiah, moves in the inverse direction: marked 'lento teneramente e con melancolia' at its start, it moves to anguished energy. The Latin text asks why a chosen vine, planted and carefully tended, has turned into bitterness. 'I did my work carefully, why is this happening to me?' is the question posed by this motet, which could apply to any careful craftsman who humbly laboured in the vineyards. (Poulenc was a vine-grower at Noizay, where grapes in his garden produced a light, golden wine.) The last two motets concern Christ's crucifixion. The third motet, 'Tenebrae factae sunt', assigned blame to the Jews for crucifying Jesus – the official line of the Catholic church until Vatican II absolved the Jews of this responsability: 'It became dark when the Jews had crucified Jesus, and around the ninth hour, Jesus exclaimed in a loud voice, "My God, why have you forsaken me?"' In 1938 and 1939 many Frenchmen were resisting the idea of fighting a war 'in order to save the Jews'. It was not the best time to point a finger of blame at Jews as Christ-killers. The four motets finish with the words of Jesus in the Garden of Gethsemene, 'Tristis est anima mea' (My soul is sad), declaring that 'the Son of man will be betrayed into the hands of sinners.' The composer relied on a solo soprano to express much of the anguish of this plaint.

In these liturgical works for holy week, Poulenc set the tragedy that France and the rest of Europe were experiencing in a historical, religious context. The air of sadness and defeat in these works, especially 'Tristis est anima mea', approaches the gloom of some African-American spirituals, and the impression created is of the depressed, frozen horror of Frenchmen who had experienced World War I and who now saw a second war coming. Despite the horror, Poulenc's work retained its sweetness.

Equally in the spirit of the times is 'Priez pour paix', a song that Poulenc wrote with accompaniment in four-part harmony to lines by the fifteenth-century poet Charles d'Orléans. Poulenc had found excerpts of the poem reprinted in *Le Figaro* one morning in September 1938, and decided to make a song of them, fit for a prayer from a country sanctuary.

The *Quatre Motets* and 'Priez pour paix' are the work of a composer abandoning all hope for the future of humanity. But Poulenc was still concerned with the posterity of his works and in 1939 he hastily jotted down thoughts on his songs and other works. Creating this *Journal de mes mélodies* was triggered by a horrible radio performance of his songs on 3 November 1939, as the first entry indicates: 'Horrible day!!! A lady on the radio has just meowed for an entire fifteen minutes, melodies which just might be by me!' Aghast at this intepretation at a time when he felt insecure about his future, Poulenc set about describing how his songs should be interpreted. The *Journal*, to which he added intermittently, became a place for recollections, ideas and anecdotes. Had he not felt *in extremis* in 1939, he would not have begun it. In his works of the late 1930s, Poulenc who was not at all socially committed, clearly feared the worst.

5

Poulenc's War 1940–5

Poulenc avoided the sight of German troops marching beneath Paris's Arc de Triomphe by staying as much as possible in his country estate at Noizay during World War II.

It will never be known how much I owe to Eluard, how much I owe to Bernac. It's thanks to them that lyricism penetrated into my vocal works. The first, because of the warmth of his images. The second, thanks to his admirable musical understanding and above all what he taught me about the art of singing.

Francis Poulenc, *Journal de mes mélodies*

Poulenc's War 1940–5

With the oncoming war blotted out of his consciousness as much as possible, Poulenc's most acute worry at the end of the 1930s was his increasing obsession with being a 'great' composer. He wrote to Marie-Blanche de Polignac:

> *One must be resigned and well-behaved if one wants to be a great musician. And I am currently haunted by precisely this delirium of greatness. Therefore I must bear the consequences.*

Yet an important interruption loomed, World War II, which threatened to be as distracting to his work as World War I had been. Poulenc spent the latter part of 1939 anxiously waiting to be called up for military service, confessing that the only thing that it pained him to leave was his piano. During the 'hesitation waltz' that marked France's entry into the war, Poulenc was too apprehensive to write music. Instead he reorchestrated *Les Biches*, in order to leave it in perfect form in case the worst happened, and revised his Sextet for piano, flute, oboe, clarinet, bassoon and horn, partially composed in 1932.

First performed in December 1940, the Sextet extends the expertise evident in Poulenc's 1926 Trio for oboe, bassoon, and piano. In three movements, Allegro vivace, Divertissement and Finale, the new version of the Sextet was a warmingly convivial project. The first movement resembles a toccata, with a Stravinskian classicism to the fore. The second movement, marked *andantino*, is equally classical in form, a slow–fast–slow structure, and the *prestissimo* finale is a variation on a rondo. What creates the interest of the work is not its slightly altered classical framework, but rather the heartfelt romantic melodies which Poulenc hung on this bare-bones structure.

The work not only offers opportunities for daredevil virtuoso pianism, but also for emotionally charged statements by the wind players. When the Sextet is played by first-rate instrumentalists who have a touch of the poet, like the French horn player André Cazalet, the work's qualities are well conveyed, but when the Sextet is played too 'ensemble', so that the individual egos of the performers are not audible, the work loses a dimension. In this sense the Sextet may be Poulenc's work most influenced by jazz, not because of the way it sounds, but because of the liberty and individuality needed to play it.

Poulenc also read Bossuet, La Fontaine and Baudelaire to pass the time until he was finally called up as a private (second class). He went to Cahors with a regiment of farmers and, after the French capitulation, he returned to his country home at Noizay where he spent the rest of the war years.

Poulenc's reaction to the war and German Occupation was self-centred. As a composer, he needed valued colleagues and friends like Darius Milhaud and Wanda Landowska for their advice and encouragement, and he was distressed by their forced exile. The German occupants ransacked and destroyed the library Wanda Landowska had created at St-Leu, solely because the harpsichordist was born a Polish Jew; they also visited the Paris archives of HMV to destroy every record she and other Jewish musicians had made. This sort of detailed obliteration of culture revolted Poulenc. He did nothing to risk his life and career in order to prevent it, but neither did he profit grossly from the arrival of the Germans.

In 1940 Poulenc wrote to the exiled Milhaud that during his absence for military service, his Touraine home, had been pillaged. This was false. No doubt Poulenc wanted to show solidarity with Milhaud, as a fellow sufferer, although the truth was otherwise. He also told Milhaud that he still had hopes to be able to tour America in 1941–2. He had had some doubts about returning to occupied Paris, but Georges Auric urged him to do so quickly. Poulenc bragged to Auric that if he needed a visa, he could always ask his good friend the pianist Walter Gieseking, who was 'Kommandantur' in occupied France.

Even though he was not guilty of some of his colleagues' more heinous deeds of the German Occupation, Poulenc's attitude towards collaboration was complex and shifting. Others of his friends were more clear-cut: Arthur Honegger continued writing as usual, con-

tributing articles to collaborationist journals, and travelled to Vienna twice in 1941, invited by the Germans to celebrate the 150th anniversary of Mozart's death. By contrast, Louis Durey retired completely from composing during the Occupation, preferring to edit music rather than write anything new at this tragic time for his country. Poulenc's activities were somewhere between these two extremes. He recorded and performed his works plentifully in occupied Paris, yet he avoided some of Cocteau's more gratuitous social contacts with Nazis which were so criticized after the war; nor did not share Cocteau's early moments of fascination for Hitler's charisma.

Bernac's actions were brave from the beginning. Unlike most noted French singers, he refused to sing for the Nazi-controlled propaganda radio, and thereby lost an important source of income for five years; he subsisted by teaching during the war years. Poulenc later claimed that his wartime recitals with Bernac were devoted only to French music. In fact, the programmes of the Poulenc–Bernac concerts in occupied Paris contained the works of German composers such as Liszt and Schumann, as well as Stravinsky.

Opposite, called up in 1940, at a time of general mobilization, Poulenc was reassured about France's disastrous loss by his fellow soldiers, simple countrymen whose company Poulenc always favoured for affairs of the heart.

André Halimi's *Chantons sous l'Occupation*, a study of the arts in Nazi-occupied Paris, states that for most Parisians, during the war it was business as usual. Poulenc started out more or less in this vein. He agreed to write his first film score, for a screenplay by Jean Giraudoux, *La Duchesse de Langeais*, after a story by Balzac; the film had its première in Paris in March 1942. Later, Poulenc wrote stage music for a Jean Anouilh play, *Le Voyageur sans bagages*, and adapted his music for the screen when the film was made in 1944. In 1941 Paul Valéry sent Poulenc a book inscribed 'To Francis Poulenc or the good collaboration', in thanks for a new song, *Colloque*, which the composer had set to a Valéry poem. However, soon collaboration of any kind did not look good: by 1943 the Vichy racial laws had settled in and large numbers of people disappeared to concentration camps.

Poulenc gradually found that the absence of Jews made French musical life less exciting. In October 1943 he told André Jolivet, 'Without being philosemite, I must say that Jewish yeast is indispensable for making the custard batter rise in the concert halls. Besides, I prefer my *Mouvements perpétuels* played by Horowitz than

To his credit, Poulenc was not thrilled by the fascist aesthetic, unlike some Frenchmen like Jean Cocteau and Maurice Sachs, who found erotic S-and-M excitement in the Nazi jackboot.

by Lucienne Delforge.' After three years of life without Jewish musicians, from Pierre Monteux to Reynaldo Hahn, French music was drab indeed. As Poulenc indicated, in a performance the Opéra orchestra could no longer be relied upon since the empty places of Jews and other prisoners had not been filled.

At the age of sixty-seven, Marya Freund was deported to Drancy, but transferred to the camp's hospital after intervention by Marie-Blanche de Polignac and the soprano Germaine Lubin. Both had influence with the Nazi occupants and attended receptions hosted by them, which caused some problems, at least for Lubin, after the war was over. The elderly Freund managed to escape from the hospital and was sheltered by the pianist Irène Aïtoff, escaping to the free zone for the rest of the war. Other friends were less fortunate; the composer and sculptor Fernand Ochsé and his wife Louise were deported to Auschwitz and killed.

Amid all this tragedy, Poulenc managed to write a gracefully sentimental waltz, 'Les Chemins de l'amour'. The song was written for the popular soprano Yvonne Printemps, as had been the Renaissance-style ballad, 'À Sa Guitare'. 'Les Chemins de l'amour' originated in a play by Jean Anouilh, and the willfully banal words create a fond homage to a waltz tradition. Yvonne Printemps's delicious sense of irony was honed during performances with Sacha Guitry and Pierre Fesnay, her first and second husbands respectively. Her lightness and freshness owed a lot to her odd vocal emission – she said, 'I'm a mezzo-soprano who goes up and who goes down ...' Few among the multitude of singers who tackle 'Les Chemins de l'amour' really understand the operetta tradition (at which the song was a self-conscious knowing wink) and how to convey the necessary lightness and humour.

In the middle of the war, Poulenc wrote one of his most popular and accessible groups of songs, *Banalités*, to poems by Apollinaire. The delightfully idiotic 'Voyage à Paris' declares goofily 'Paris jolie!' This was meant to sound like a parody of a travel brochure. Poulenc said of *Banalités*, 'I tried, using the inspiration of Matisse's drawings, to go from complex things to a simple line', as he had done when composing the *Cinq Poèmes de Paul Eluard*. In one of the *Banalités* songs, 'Hôtel', the hotel room filled with cigarette smoke and the languid narrator are scenically evoked as in a painting by Vuillard or

Opposite, during the German Occupation, Poulenc looked back to different times of struggle – the fatal tussle of Apollinaire (here drawn in uniform by Picasso) with the demons of World War I.

PICASSO

Dufy. The lazy plea from the workaholic Poulenc, 'I don't want to work, I want to smoke,' was heartfelt. He also set three more poems of Louise de Vilmorin, grouped under the title *Métamorphoses* (1943): 'Reine des Mouettes', 'C'est ainsi que tu es' and 'Paganini'. The first song was as flighty and insubstantial as the second was deeply expressive. The rapid pace of 'Paganini', however, with its virtuoso explosiveness, was later considered by Poulenc a failure, at best a melody that should serve as a 'trampoline' to a more lyric song, not constituting the end of a cycle.

The six *Chansons villageoises* (1942) were a weightier response to the war years. These songs attempted to find a kernel of French experience that had lasted through the ages, a national approach to life that is constant. Roots in the Touraine countryside gave Poulenc a sense of stability, and during his brief military service in 1939, he was comforted by the presence of country fellows also serving, and this cycle of village songs reflects the composer's admiration for non-sophisticates. The music in these songs is very challenging – Poulenc's melody ranging up and down the scale, taxing even the most accomplished singers.

The composer saw these *Chansons villageoises* as appropriate for a solid Verdi baritone. Heroic lung power was part of his original conception and operatic baritones like Gabriel Bacquier have made a speciality of the cycle. Poulenc said that the singer at the first performance in June 1943, opera baritone Roger Bourdin, was fine, but that he lacked physical bulk. If Bourdin, who had an opera career, was insufficiently heroic, the light-voiced Bernac could only sing the cycle with piano, since the orchestration drowned him out entirely. This desire for a Verdian voice was a striving for power by Poulenc, not suggested in the original texts by the folkloric poet Maurice Fombeure.

Poulenc said that one song from the cycle, 'Le Mendiant', was 'very inspired' by Mussorgsky's *Songs and Dances of Death*. It is a cry for compassion, made against the 'damned race that feels no pity'. Pierre Bernac commented that, 'This poem, violently vengeful and vindictive, effectively inspired the composer to create heavy and violent music …' Folded into a cycle of largely comic folkloric numbers, 'Le Mendiant' is a musical equivalent to Victor Hugo's cries for social justice, with the narrator taking on the role of an aggrieved Quasimodo. The song was performed in public during the Occupation and its aggressive 'worm will turn' threat was the closest Poulenc came, while danger was still present, to writing music that expressed emotional rebellion akin to the French Resistance movement. Part of his humdrum daily existence was assuring that he was well-fed in the country (rich Parisians dined at black market restaurants throughout the Occupation); in August 1943 Poulenc cried with relief, 'I'm saved!' because he had succeeded in keeping the services of his cook at *Le Grand Coteau*.

The same year he ceded to the pressures of the young violinist, Ginette Neveu, to write a violin sonata; he had already made numerous attempts starting in 1918 but was never satisfied with the results. The masculine, forceful Neveu was not to be denied, and the resulting sonata was in three movements, an Allegro con fuoco, an Intermezzo and a Presto tragico. The Intermezzo was intended to be 'vaguely Spanish' and the work was dedicated to the memory of Federico García Lorca, a martyr of fascist troops, which was a daring step in wartime Paris. Although he later revised the work, Poulenc still did not like the sound of the solo violin, and considered that the only idiomatic parts of his sonata were those which had been suggested by Ginette Neveu. The violinist's manly decisiveness may have reminded Poulenc of the late Raymonde Linossier.

Poulenc surprised a number of his friends by accepting to write a ballet for the first time since *Les Biches* of twenty years previously. *Les Animaux modèles*, written for the Paris Opéra, was based on episodes from his beloved La Fontaine. Poulenc asked Eluard to give him ideas for the ballet's title, to which Eluard replied that he could not stand La Fontaine 'and his fables so brutally imposed, sweated by heart. Their morality is a prison which I don't want to penetrate any more.' Poulenc seemed to need this strict morality more than Eluard who, as a communist, was a active member of the French Resistance.

Poulenc chose to set six of La Fontaine's fables: 'L'Ours et les deux Compagnons', 'La Cigale et la Fourmi', 'Le Lion amoureux', 'L'Homme entre deux ages et ses deux maîtresses', 'La Mort et le Bûcheron' and 'Les Deux Coqs'. Poulenc invented a new twist: the animals in the fables would regain human appearance. The prodigal

Cigale becoming a ballerina down on her luck, the Lion amoureux a bad-boy seducer. The ballet, set in a farm on a sunny summer's day, begins with the peasants leaving for the fields and ends with their return for lunch. A blessing is sung as the final curtain falls, a scene inspired by the paintings of the seventeenth-century artists Les Frères Le Nain.

Les Animaux modèles was written in the form of a suite, as *Les Biches* had been. But the mood in the later work is far more sombre: peasant prayers have the solemn urgency of the *Litanies à la Vierge noire.* A rare moment of comic relief was a sprightly java danced by the Lion amoureux. Poulenc's romantic term for men with whom he had relationships was 'my peasant', and his obsessional interest in peasants and their lifestyle reached its peak in this work. In France, the Maréchal Pétain led a revival of worship of the earth and the French peasant, and in so far as *Les Animaux modèles* abided by these ideals, it is a Pétainist work.

Poulenc was fascinated with the 'common folk', not just as a source of sexual partners. He preferred taking a second class seat for the train from Paris to his country home in Touraine, because he found the people more interesting to watch than in the snooty first class. In July 1943, while on holiday in Corrèze, Poulenc reported to friends:

I eat correct and rather copious meals in a seedy dive where a Paris gym teacher in a little bathing slip shows off his muscles to a hairdresser from Antoine's, timid and swooning, all in front of her husband, a bit long in the tooth and concerned ... under the disapproving glance of Raymond, who can't see why I find this bloke so appealing!!!

Some found it odd that Poulenc waited for the German Occupation before writing another ballet; yet the composer's defenders pointed to the fact that he incorporated in the movement 'Les Deux Coqs' an old French anti-German song, 'Non, non, vous n'aurez pas notre Alsace-Lorraine'. Furthermore, the première of *Animaux modèles* was conducted by Roger Désormière, who was active in the Resistance. To these points it must be added that the ballet was choreographed by the ballet's director Serge Lifar, a great chum of the Nazi occupants.

Whatever the political timing, Poulenc was musically ready for the challenge of *Animaux modèles*: since writing *Les Biches*, he had gained practical experience in writing for string sections in works such as *Sécheresses* and the Organ Concerto. As if reminding himself of his musical preparation, Poulenc quoted a number of his own melodies in the score of his new ballet: the songs 'Hôtel' and 'Sanglots' from *Banalités* are recognizable; moments of the ballet recall *Les Biches* and the Organ Concerto. It was as if Poulenc had arrived at a stage as a composer where he was no longer obliged to quote others and could now steal from himself. He placed *Animaux modèles* precisely in his musical output: 'I consider it as a crossroads-work in which are juxtaposed the style of my choral works of 1938 to 1940, a last bit of eroticism, and finally, a more complex harmonic sense which I had in different areas from 1940 to 1950.'

Despite its lush orchestration, death is very much present in the ballet, which Poulenc dedicated to Raymonde Linossier. The movement, 'La Mort et le Bûcheron' ('Death and the Woodcutter'), contains a deliberate reference to Schubert's 'Death and the Maiden' quartet, but in Poulenc's ballet, Death *is* the Maiden. Poulenc's more complex musical messages were not easily perceived by some listeners. When his teacher Charles Koechlin praised the new 'very amusing' ballet, Poulenc, who valued the moral aspect of La Fontaine, as well as his status as a poet for children, replied plaintively that his work had serious parts, too. Koechlin was not the only listener to skate over the ominous aspects of Poulenc's work. Wartime articles presented the musician as a jovial country composer, seemingly undisturbed by the presence of an enemy occupant in his country. The novelist Colette reviewed *Les Animaux modèles* for an arts magazine, describing Poulenc as 'a big boney guy, rural, merry ... Surrounded by his vines, Poulenc lives in a big, airy house, where he makes and drinks his wine.' Colette encouraged a myth of Poulenc as a country composer, inspired by the *terroir* (heartland). Poulenc was always eager to deny this; in fact, the countryside bored him to tears and he only went there in order to find the calm to write.

Listening to *Les Animaux modèles*, Arthur Honegger made peace with Poulenc's aesthetic, saying that the influences previously audible in Poulenc, such as Chabrier, Satie and Stravinsky, were now

completely assimilated. Still, Poulenc's quest for greatness was not sated. By 1943 the composer was increasingly frustrated with the German Occupation: absent friends, compromised social life, and moral choices to be made all the time, angered him. This irritation manifested itself in the clandestine choral work, *Figure humaine*, written for performance after the war. Poulenc was terrified to learn that Raymond had almost been arrested by the Germans and sent to a forced labour camp; although his boyfriend was safe, Poulenc never forgot his fright at the near-tragedy.

Opposite, Poulenc was a longtime friend of the novelist Colette (1873–1954). He hoped to work with her on a 1931 film, with 'very beautiful actors, for it's a film of incandescent love,' but the project was stillborn.

His half-hidden expressions of rage in *Chansons villageoises* and *Les Animaux modèles* no longer sufficed. *Figure humaine* is more uncompromising than *Animaux modèles*, as is evident in the direction that it be sung through teeth 'clenched with hatred'. Poulenc later claimed that the idea to write this work came 'after a pilgrimage to Rocamadour'. The truth is more banal. At a concert in March 1943, in which *Sept Chansons* was performed, Henri Screpel, director of a French record publisher, La Compagnie des Discophiles, approached Poulenc, asking the composer to make a choral setting of Eluard's poem 'Liberté', for a recording. In July Poulenc wrote a full-scale cantata in six weeks using eight of Eluard's poems: 'De tous les printemps du monde', 'En chantant les servantes s'élancent', 'Aussi bas que le silence', 'Toi ma patiente', 'Riant du ciel et des planètes', 'Le jour m'étonne et la nuit me fait peur', 'La ménace sous le ciel rouge', and 'Liberté'. The first and last poems in *Figure humaine* can be described as 'Resistance' music, with the statement, 'Of all the world's springtimes, this one is the ugliest', and the ultimate cry, 'Liberté!'.

Figure humaine was written for a twelve-part double choir, and despite the challenges of writing for such a dense vocal texture, Poulenc triumphed with an art of refined polyphony. Some of the movements sound almost like an organ, others like orchestral instruments: there are snatches of fugues and vivid scherzo passages. Particularly impressive is the vastly challenging final poem, 'Liberté': a long work of twenty-one quatrains, which, like Cocteau's *Toréador*, risked monotony. However, Poulenc's art had advanced mightily in twenty years and he stated modestly that in order to set 'Liberté' it was only necessary to know Eluard's rhythm as well as possible. The vocal modulations were gymnastic and the inflections were of great precision, ending with a triumphal final chord marked '*fff*, explosive, very large', in which the voices are spread richly over four octaves. Poulenc wrote spectacular high notes for the soprano soloists at the very end, underlining its operatic nature. *Figure humaine* was composed with a harmonic ideal in mind, with a huge variety of dynamics and emotional expression. Its vocal difficulty makes performances very rare, yet Poulenc refused to add instrumental accompaniment to his work, saying that the independence of voices without any instrumental support was part of the message of his music.

Figure humaine was dedicated to Pablo Picasso, 'whose work and life I admire'. Poulenc performed the work alone at the piano, during evenings at Marie-Laure de Noailles's home and at a special hearing for Picasso and Eluard in the winter of 1943. Ironically, as this chorus was Poulenc's hidden bow to the French Resistance, Picasso's role during the occupation of Paris has been questioned. As a rich foreigner in wartime Paris, the artist lived relatively well, paying no apparent heed to events. When his friend Max Jacob wrote a pleading letter from prison, Picasso did not reply. His main virtue was his concentration on creative productivity at all costs. As for Poulenc, the day the American troops arrived at Noizay, he placed *Figure humaine* on the lectern of his studio, near a French flag. He hoped that *Figure humaine* and *Les Mamelles de Tirésias* would be taken as 'a sufficient Frenchman's tribute'.

In 1954 Poulenc said that the première of *Figure humaine* took place in London in January 1945, before the end of the war, explaining that he was able to attend the last rehearsals by boarding a military plane crossing the Channel. These recollections are inexact: the British première of *Figure humaine* was in fact in March of 1945. (In January Poulenc *did* go to England, but to perform his Concerto for Two Pianos with Benjamin Britten, which might have seemed a less heroic reason for travel, later on.) After the first Paris performance in May 1947, *Figure humaine* was not heard again in France until 1959, when Poulenc himself programmed it in a evening of his works. The *a cappella* harmonies were too difficult for French choirs, but in America, where the choral art was better developed, the work won an immediate popularity.

Opposite, Picasso furnished a wartime example for Poulenc by sticking to his work, oblivious to the tragedies around him; his longtime friend Max Jacob died in a French concentration camp without Picasso's lifting a finger to help.

The anecdotes surrounding *Figure humaine* have distracted attention from another fine choral work from 1944, *Un Soir de neige*,

A cry against war: Picasso's *Guernica* (1937). Poulenc was a constant admirer of Picasso's art and of his life.

a setting of four poems by Paul Eluard for six vocal parts *a cappella.* Poulenc's imagination had been working on the theme of a winter voyage in recollection of his boyhood afternoons spent at the piano with Schubert's *Die Winterreise.* To the strong and moving poems, Poulenc wrote music of less sweetness than in *Figure humaine,* with a Northern European flavour. Its four movements are 'Des Grandes Cuillers de neige', 'La Bonne Neige', 'Bois meurtri' and 'La Nuit le Froid la Solitude'. The singers hurry by, as if too cold to tarry. The winters at the end of the Second World War *were* exceedingly cold, even for the privileged few like Poulenc, who had no problems with fuel. *Un Soir de neige* is preferable in its concentrated version for six voices, rather than expanded for full choir, as it gives the impression of a valiant, lonely struggle against physical hardships and the elements, without the aid of strength in numbers. In its compassion for the sufferings of wartime, the work may be compared to Debussy's song inspired by World War I, 'Noël des enfants qui n'ont plus de maison'.

Another paradigmatic work during the Occupation was the song 'C', to a poem by Louis Aragon. The poet was an ardent communist and member of the Resistance during the war who, like Eluard, defended Stalinism. After the death of his wife Elsa, however, the elderly Aragon became an outspoken advocate of gay liberation, appearing at Gay Pride parades in a pink convertible, surrounded by ephebes.

The poem 'C' is a consciously archaic and slightly precious evocation of old France, using the medieval convention of an identical rhyme at the end of each line. The poem mixed images of chivalry with contemporary war-torn France. 'C' spoke eloquently for its time, and Poulenc's setting was of a rare lyric beauty, particularly in its plaint for 'O ma France, o ma délaissé'. In 1945 the critic Frederick Goldbeck reproached Poulenc for setting Aragon's poem in an atmosphere of nineteenth-century Romanticism. The composer replied that the poem itself was highly romantic, 'much closer to Musset than to Baudelaire', and that compared to Eluard, Aragon was a 'lightweight' poet. More enthused was Koechlin, who told the composer that 'C' 'breathes the soul of our wounded homeland'.

Like everything else, classical song programmes followed the course of history. After D-Day Poulenc wrote to Bernac, who was mulling over a selection of Schubert songs for the pair's Winter 1944 recital in Paris, making the astute comment that the next year there would be no concerts or it would be impossible to sing in German, so it would be prudent to consider songs by Borodin and Milhaud.

In November 1944, Milhaud wrote in *Modern Music* magazine, 'I know now that Poulenc, Louis Durey, Georges Auric, and Roger Désormière were active in the Resistance.' In Poulenc's case, this statement was untrue, and a generous exaggeration. Milhaud knew that Poulenc had paid special attention to his mother who, widowed during the war, lived alone in Marseilles and pined for her exiled son. As soon as the war ended, Poulenc made strenuous efforts to ease Milhaud's return to France, publishing an article praising his œuvre, and arranging for concerts of Milhaud's works.

The war years had saddened Milhaud, and he did not come back to France right away, despite Poulenc's efforts to get him back to Paris. When he did return it was in poor health – advancing rheumatoid arthritis soon left him wheelchair-bound or bedridden. As professor at the Conservatoire, a role he assumed in 1947, he was sometimes obliged to give classes from his bed in his apartment on the boulevard de Clichy. Although Milhaud was still a fine musical thinker, he distressed some friends by his seemingly undiscriminating urge to produce.

In his country retreat with Raymond, Poulenc was also hampered by attacks of rheumatism and arthritis, which he treated by homeopathy and allopathy. He grumbled about how La Touraine 'killed' him: 'I've always worked here as in a prison, dreaming of enchanted lands like Monte Carlo, Nogent, the boulevard de la Chapelle, etc.' As the war drew to a close, Poulenc was slightly ashamed that Noizay was intact when many of his friends had suffered so greatly. In 1945 he harmonized eight choral *Chansons françaises*; these archaic songs, teeming with pretty maidens and handsome labourers, are monotonous, repetitive and long. Poulenc's attempt to be a national composer backfired because, unlike the *Chansons villageoises*, there was no hidden agenda to the folkloric texts.

Comforted by Raymond's presence, which Poulenc likened to that of 'a faithful dog', he took up a project he had put aside at the start of the war, an operatic version of Apollinaire's *Les Mamelles de Tirésias,* in which he hoped to integrate melancholy with wild farce. 'Mamelles'

ABRÉGÉ DU
CAPITAL
STALINE
TRAITE
DE
SCIENCE
OCCULTE

in French is not 'breasts' as has been politely translated but rather 'teats', as on a female animal. He wanted to make listeners laugh, and yet offer moments of tender lyricism. The two act opera runs under an hour in performance. A woman in Zanzibar, Thérèse, decides to be a feminist and work at a job like a man. Her breasts, toy balloons, fly up to the roof. She grows a beard, and goes on a rampage, tying up her husband, who is dressed in women's clothes, and convinces other women to stop child-bearing. Apollinaire called his play a *drame surréaliste*. Yet he had written most of it in 1903, well before the official Surrealist movement began. Apollinaire shared with Poulenc a nursery ideal of sexuality, appreciating the time in childhood when gender is irrelevant.

Opposite, this slightly prophetic caricature of the poet Louis Aragon from 1936 shows him as a bejewelled and long-fingernailed mystic, and an admirer of Marxism and the occult sciences.

A key to Poulenc's serious involvement in this work was the piano part for the *entracte*, which is full of chords out of Grieg and Tchaikovsky. As in *Aubade*, Poulenc wrote the piano part as if he would be performing it himself, with many charming personal touches and a particular gusto. A dazzling variety of dance music accompanies all of this hysteria, including waltzes, polkas and Spanish steps. Yet deep emotion inhabits the music, and Poulenc later claimed that he wrote *Mamelles* in the same style as his *Stabat Mater* of 1950. Further, he claimed that *Mamelles* should be sung exactly like a work by Verdi, and that its music, set to a Latin text, would make a fine sacred oratorio. Poulenc's subject matter was drab demography, but his style was operatic and Italian. *Les Mamelles* switched at a moment's notice from popular, catchy dance tunes to beautiful Italianate operatic writing.

The work opens with the *Directeur* addressing the public in full-throated Italian vocalism, reminiscent of the Mandarin's cry of 'Popolo di Pekino!' in Puccini's *Turandot*. There is no overture, and a preliminary scene by Apollinaire was cut by Poulenc; he may have felt that the initial scene, in which the poet evoked wartime ('we were there, dying the death of stars') would be too tragic. In Apollinaire's play, after Thérèse declares her feminist ambitions, she 'lets out a great scream' and opens her blouse. Her breasts, blue and red balloons, fly upward, held aloft by two strings. Instead of Apollinaire's scream, Poulenc had Thérèse emit a pleasurable sigh, 'ah-hah'. She lightly breaks into a floating waltz when her breast-balloons fly aloft. Her high-flying coloratura is like that of Marguérite in Gounod's *Faust*.

Les Mamelles de Tirésias was an integrated surrealist masterpiece, akin to Marcel Duchamp's last work *Large Glass*, into which previous styles and approaches were incorporated to create strange, new messages. In Apollinaire's work, the weirdest things happen, with total naturalness and nonchalance. It has an infantile humour, reminiscent of the strident, absurdist farces of Alfred Jarry when Thérèse's husband called her a *merdecine* (doctor-shit), which a policement interprets as *mère des cygnes* (mother of swans). The lines, 'Listen, French people, to the lessons of the war, and make children, ye who hardly ever used to', were used once by Apollinaire in his play, but Poulenc repeated them again and again, adding a final chorus influenced by the ending of Verdi's *Falstaff* to further emphasize the point. Poulenc's fertility message was forward-looking, but another aspect of *Les Mamelles* focused on the recent past: the baby son of Thérèse's husband threatens to denounce and blackmail his father for imaginary crimes (in Act II, scene iv). This must have struck a chord in France, so soon after the German occupation when some children did indeed denounce their parents to the Nazi authorities.

In 1945, Poulenc had had an affair with a 39-year-old woman, Frédérique, a cousin of Richard Chanlaire's sister-in-law, whom he had known since the mid 1920s. Their daughter, Marie-Ange, was born in 1946. Fathering a child with a woman was not unheard of in Poulenc's circle of gay friends – Cocteau was rumoured to have done so once or twice in fits of pique after unsuccessful gay romances. Poulenc dedicated a song from *Tel Jour, telle nuit* to Frédérique, who has wished to preserve her privacy and anonymity. The same is true of Marie-Ange, who had a career as a classical ballet dancer. Poulenc was caring and solicitous about his daughter, presenting himself as her godfather and writing letters to the young girl in which he would encourage her to learn her catechism. Poulenc admired her dream of becoming a dancer, and when she was ten, he asked the director of the Paris Opéra, Georges Hirsch, for advice about her dance education. He remained friends with Frédérique until his death.

Mamelles was finished in 1945, but its staging had to wait because the former director of the Opéra-Comique was fired, after the Liberation of Paris, for having collaborated, and a soprano was yet to be found to sing the difficult role of Thérèse. Poulenc approached the young lyric soprano Geori Boué, and when she turned him down he discovered a soprano, Denise Duval, who had sung at the Folies Bergères; he called Duval 'lovely as the day, chic on earth, a voice of gold', and took her to parties, dressed in robes lent by his friend Christian Dior. Poulenc ardently praised her as 'a new Fanny Heldy', the 1920s Opéra-Comique star, but Duval fascinated influential Paris

The charm and ardent singing of the chic young soprano Denise Duval (b. 1921), here pictured in her role as Thérèse/Tirésias in *Les Mamelles de Tirésias* (1947), soon won her Poulenc's affection.

Duval dans les mamelles

snobs even before they knew she could sing. Duval always denied rumours that she and Poulenc were lovers, calling him 'ugly as a louse'. Poulenc suggested in 1947 that she was more attached to her dressmaker: 'Christian Dior dresses her, and that's not all he does!'

Les Mamelles was given its première on 3 June 1947 at the Opéra-Comique, in a double bill, bizarrely, with Puccini's *La Bohème*. Some audiences who came to see a conventional production of *La Bohème* were outraged by Poulenc's wild farce with its sets and costumes by Erté, the famous and fey stage designer of the Folies Bergères. Others felt that the wild high spirits were out of place in sombre post-war Paris. Poulenc's music seemed to suggest that Paris had not changed, but for some people, it had changed irrevocably.

But most critics cheered; Paul Le Flem wrote that the gravity of *Mamelles*'s prologue 'seemed to announce some austere subject. A feint. Like his poet, Poulenc reserves his pirouettes for later … as if he is according a few moments of contemplation in memory of Apollinaire, before following his leader into the land of improbability.' The juxtaposition of *Mamelles* with the Paris première of *Figure humaine* in September 1947, impressed many listeners. The critic Henri Hell wrote that any composer who could produce two such different works as *Mamelles* and *Figure humaine*, 'each perfect in its genre', had to be termed 'a born musician'. Admiration for Poulenc's achievement was steadily growing.

6

The Road to the Carmelites 1946–53

Jean de Brunhoff's illustration of the Elephant King recumbent with a bellyache after eating a bad mushroom; the story of Babar inspired one of Poulenc's most delightful works.

Operetta amuses me, but I have no talent for writing one. Alas, this genre has strayed and become bastardized, because let's not forget, in order to succeed in it, one needs special talents, like the great Messager (yes, Messager was a great musician) or closer to our day, Reynaldo Hahn and Louis Beydts. You can't improvise the skill needed to write an operetta. So, the second act finale of Mamelles, *which has the false aspect of an operetta, is not an operetta finale. It's too dry, too grimacing, and not as gay as all that.*

Francis Poulenc,
Entretiens avec Claude Rostand

The Road to the Carmelites 1946–53

For Poulenc, the war was really over when he could return to international touring. In January 1945 he and Bernac gave a series of song recitals at the Wigmore Hall in London. On 7 January, at the first concert that programmed music by Fauré, Debussy, and Poulenc, the audience rose to welcome them, and Bernac was so moved that instead of starting to sing, he wept. Poulenc did not waste any time in getting down to serious, career-building work: the first all-Poulenc concert was held 27 April 1945, at the Salle Gaveau in Paris. This concert was a great success, although Poulenc was sick with nerves before and after the performance. To friends, Poulenc crowed about his own self-discipline and avoidance of trouble during the dangerous years, as opposed to some other, more foolish colleagues. He wrote to the anti-fascist composer Luigi Dallapiccola about how he had prudently avoided compromising himself during the Occupation, and how Bernac had refused to sing on Nazi-controlled radio. Poulenc was so conscious of appearing on the right side after the war that he publicly dedicated a song to Dallapiccola in 1946, without even telling the Italian he had done so. This could be seen as evidence of a guilty conscience at having been a non-hero during a time of moral challenge, or a late reaction against the crimes committed.

Honours were forthcoming. A friend, the Swiss-born painter Roger Wild, suggested to Paul Eluard that he might write a poem in homage of Poulenc. The poet, who had apparently never had the notion to do so, complied in the spring of 1945. The lines, 'Francis, I didn't hear myself … Francis I owe it to you to have heard myself' are often quoted in books on Poulenc. The composer ardently urged 'for my future glory' that this poem be included in a collection, only half in jest, but Eluard omitted to do so until he died in 1952. In Paris, where so often friendships are based on mutual flattery and favours, this was a significant snub.

Opposite, the poet Paul Eluard, whom Poulenc loved, was not the somewhat flabby, pasty, diehard communist who often made headlines in France, but rather the ageless lyric poet of love.

VOIR

One advantage of resuming foreign travel was commissions from abroad. The BBC clamoured for Poulenc to finish his *L'Histoire de Babar* in its piano version. Other concert works for children, like Prokofiev's *Peter and the Wolf* and Britten's *Young People's Guide to the Orchestra*, have been didactic in intent. Poulenc, by contrast, was moved entirely by the pleasure principal – he wanted to hear children crow with delight.

To friends, Poulenc described *Babar* as 'Eighteen Glimpses at the Tail of a Young Elephant', a joke that had been inspired by the title of a recent work by Messiaen, *Vingt Regards sur l'Enfant Jésus.* (In French the word for 'tail', 'queue', is also the word for 'prick'; and in this subtitle the composer was referring to a certain ribald charm that the work has for adults, as well as pleasing young listeners.) Babar arrives at the big city and envies the well-dressed people he sees – 'Happily, a very rich old lady who loved little elephants very much, hands over her wallet to please him. Babar says, "Merci, Madame."' As narrated by Peter Ustinov on the EMI recording, this episode seems amusingly illicit, as if Poulenc's elephant were a gigolo.

Poulenc knew that little children adore money and cakes, appetites which he shared, and the Viennese dance music at the point when Babar buys baked goods for Arthur and Céleste could only have been

written by a pastry fiend. Poulenc also relished infantile humour: when the Elephant King in *Babar* eats a bad mushroom, a pachydermic stomach-ache begins; the music starts portentously in a Richard Straussian manner, culminating in a noisy drumroll of flatulent diarrhoea. Only a humorous Frenchman obsessed with his own digestion could have created such a musical joke, which was worthy of the repertoire of the turn-of-the-century cabaret artiste 'Le Pétomane'. To complement this low humour, when Babar marries Queen Céleste, Poulenc provided touching, noble music for the ceremony. The narrator calls out 'Mariage de Babar!', 'Couronnement de Babar!' with rapt adulation. In performance, the nonagenarian Swiss tenor Hugues

The immortal Babar drawings by de Brunhoff epitomized Poulenc's often infantile approach to adult matters: *opposite*, Babar as gigolo with the little old lady, *right*, Babar marries his queen, Céleste.

Cuénod called out these subtitles like an ancient major domo proud still to be part of the game. In *Babar* Poulenc used his own works as sources. Dance music akin to the ending of *Le Bal masqué* follows the coronation, and the song 'Hôtel' from *Banalités* is quoted when Babar and Céleste gaze languidly at the starry sky. Poulenc called this passage 'a chaste night of love for the use of children'. In 1959, occupied with other tasks, Poulenc chose the composer Jean Françaix to orchestrate *Babar*.

Despite the ease in writing the music for *L'Histoire de Babar*, composing had not become a simpler task for Poulenc. He took four years to write the song 'Montparnasse', to a poem by Guillaume Apollinaire, which was grouped with another Apollinaire song, 'Hyde Park', in 1945; two more songs from the same source followed in 1946, 'Le Pont' and 'Un Poème', all songs which are distinguished by their ambitious, atmospheric piano parts. The nature of 'Un Poème' is elliptical, Webern-like; the song tells of a solitary, ghost-like person, and although it was only seventeen measures long, it managed to evoke silence and space when performed, as the composer directed, 'excessively slowly'. Typically, 'Un Poème' ends with a sweet-sounding piano chord that 'resolves' the stylishly modern-sounding explorations that preceded it.

In 1946 Poulenc set a poem by Raymond Radiguet, 'Paul et Virginie', a portrait of breathless, youthful yearning which is as brief as was Radiguet's life. Another setting, from 1947, of Eluard's poem '... Mais Mourir', adds yet another to Poulenc's works concerned with the theme of death. 'Hymne', from the same year, is more explicitly religious, and is a setting of Jean Racine's translation in Alexandrine verse from the Roman Breviary. It was unusual for Poulenc to present in his song repertoire a strictly religious text; he usually reserved this type of text for choral settings. The composer confessed that it was impossible to set Alexandrines to music when one did not feel them as a living rhythm, which was unfortunately his case. The stern, Jansenist prayer required restraint and nobility, and Poulenc felt that Bernac's voice was more suited to this than a choral group might have been.

By contrast, prayer is represented as meaningless in another 1947 song, Robert Desnos's 'Le Disparu', a poem which bemoans a deported friend: 'No use pleading to Saints Merry, Jacques, Gervaise and Martin ...' Desnos was a surrealist poet who died in deportation and thus contributed to Poulenc's post-war survivor's guilt; he gave the poem a highly diverse musical setting, with the piano imitating a *valse-musette*, a tolling bell and a funeral march. Poulenc wrote the Desnos song at the same time as the Racine 'Hymne', which suggests that his attitude towards religion was more complex than is generally thought. Poulenc felt an ardent need to believe, and loved church ritual, Romanesque architecture, chalices and other paraphernalia of Catholicism. Despite often referring to his father's peasant-like faith, he never quite achieved this solid assurance himself.

Poulenc tried on occasion to set poets outside his familiar circle of Apollinaire and Eluard, with varying success. *Trois Chansons de García Lorca* were first performed by Bernac and Poulenc in November 1947.

Louise de Vilmorin (1902–1969), here chatting with Pierre Bernac, fascinated high society with her delivery of bitchy gossip in the tone of an innocent victim of circumstance. Poulenc admired her fragility, her limping walk, even her weak verses.

Federico García Lorca seemed an ideal poetic partner for Poulenc: he was gay (at one time in love with Salvador Dalí), and he died young, tortured and killed by Franco's troops during the Spanish Civil War. Poulenc always regretted that his Lorca settings were not Spanish enough, yet they are highly melodic and appealing, and merit more frequent performance. The composer returned hastily to his old poetic standbys. Eluard's poem, 'Main dominée par le coeur', inspired a fine new song. *Cinq poèmes de Paul Eluard* (1935) had contained a melody, 'Plume d'eau claire', with a similar vocal line, but in the later song Poulenc simplified the piano part, which clarifies the sound texture in this rapidly flowing song: a heavier accompaniment would have clogged the momentum.

His most impressive song achievement from this time is the 1948 cycle *Calligrammes*, to seven poems by Apollinaire: 'L'Espionne', 'Mutation', 'Vers Le Sud', 'Il pleut', 'La Grâce exilée', 'Aussi bien que les cigales' and 'Voyage'. Apollinaire's *Calligrammes* were printed in peculiar, innovative typographical patterns on the page, which some readers, like the practically-minded Pierre Bernac, found irritating; the patterns suggested that Apollinaire was finding new, half-hidden ways of speaking of love and sex. His poems were written between 1913 and 1917, and, meditating on these years of his youth, Poulenc took the opportunity to revisit his favourite haunts of Nogent and his adolescent friendships around the time of World War I. He made stringent efforts to unify the songs with progressive key changes from song to song, providing stricter links than in *Tel Jour, telle nuit.*

'L'Espionne' is at once about Mata Hari, and also about a woman's body, which is usually hidden but for 'one hour, one day' becomes something else. Phrases like 'les yeux bandés, prête à mourir' (blindfolded, ready to die) have more than one meaning. The first image is of the beautiful nymphomaniac spy Mata Hari blindfolded before the firing squad, the primary meaning of the word 'bandé' being bandaged; 'bandé' also refers to male sexual arousal, and dying, in Elizabethan poetry, is a metaphor for orgasm. Poulenc's lyricism, however, downplayed the cruder meanings in his setting. In 'Vers Le Sud' Apollinaire praises 'the rosebush of your body'; the following two songs are also hymns to women, and were in praise of Apollinaire's lover Marie Laurencin. Poulenc agreed that she had a lovable nature, and created a melody of Massenet-like sweetness, interrupted by many changes in tempo. The past is evoked by neo-classical figuration, and the music seems also to hesitate as the poet pauses in his memories of love during World War I.

'Aussi bien que les cigales' is one of Poulenc's strangest, yet most characteristic songs; it addressed 'people of the South of France' in the same way that *Les Mamelles* had called on the French people to reproduce. Apollinaire's text accuses the people of the south of France of knowing how to drink like cicadas do, 'but you don't know how to piss usefully, like cicadas.' When Poulenc's singer cries repeatedly, 'drink, piss, as the cicadas do!' the composer bows to the comic tradition of Chabrier, whose famous comic song honoured 'les cigales, ces bestioles'.The song concludes that by 'pissing as well as the cicadas, by singing as they do, we will have THE ADORABLE JOY OF SOLAR PEACE.' The slow and grandiose conclusion translates the large capital letters Apollinaire used for these words in his original book, ending the song with a majestic credo. The final song, 'Voyage', was for the composer one of his best: mixing emotion, silence, melancholy and affection, its calm yet intense melody was accompanied by lots of piano pedal. To Poulenc it evoked a July evening at Nogent on his grandparents' porch, when he listened to distant trains of vacationers leaving town.

More adventurous pianistically than vocally, *Calligrammes* was also a laboratory of sexual experience, offering multifarious views of human love, from operatic lyricism to sado-masochistic games. However, Poulenc also took advantage of his growing prestige to accept commissions for works which interested him less personally. He produced a *Sinfonietta* (1947) in response to a commission from the BBC radio. Poulenc was friendly with Edward Lockspeiser, the Debussy expert at the BBC, and advised him to make lots of music and 'lots of love too'. In his forties, Poulenc had settled into the role of perverse old *roué*, much like his Uncle Papoum.

Sinfonietta was written in four movements, Allegro con fuoco, Molto vivace, Andante cantabile, and Finale: prestissimo et très gai. Its source was a failed string quartet, which Poulenc had torn up and thrown into a sewer opening at the place Pereire. Parts of it were nevertheless recalled in his new *Sinfonietta*; he also quoted a number

Reconnais-toi

Cette adorable personne c'est toi

sous le grand chapeau canotier

Œil

Nez

la bouche

Voici l'ovale de ta figure

ton cou exquis

Voici enfin l'imparfaite image de ton buste adoré vu comme à travers un nuage

Un peu plus bas c'est ton cœur qui bat

of other works in the score, including *Aubade*, the Sextet, the Organ Concerto, and *Figure humaine*. Originally intended to have a classic three-movement structure, the work was inflated to four movements, perhaps to give it weight. The result is one of Poulenc's least performed large-scale works. Too pretty and discursive to stand on its own in a concert hall, *Sinfonietta* shows to what extent Poulenc needed to compose for voices, or for solo instruments. Most of the time he wrote for solo piano and was unfocused as a purely orchestral composer.

Another badly conceived commission resulted in a Sonata for cello and piano (1948). As with his violin sonata for Ginette Neveu, the Cello Sonata was the result of not wanting to refuse a famous virtuoso, Pierre Fournier. The Violin Sonata was a mess of confused statements, but at least it dared to be annoying; the Cello Sonata had not even that point of interest, but lumbered along blandly in four movements, Allegro-tempo di marcia, Cavatine, Ballabile, and Finale. One critic observed that the sonata was closer to Vincent d'Indy than to Debussy, and Renaud Machart likened the work in its melancholy to the Cello Sonata of Albéric Magnard, born some thirty years before Poulenc.

Opposite, an elegant calligram by Guillaume Apollinaire from 1915: his figured verse was the direct inspiration for Poulenc's 1948 song cycle *Calligrammes*, one of the composer's most impressive song achievements.

Poulenc pleaded successfully with his friend Marie-Blanche de Polignac to invite Raymond Destouches to her home for the first private hearing of the Cello Sonata at her home. Poulenc's society friends adored hearing him gossip about his boyfriends, but he almost never imposed them on hostesses. Unlike Cocteau, who brought his boyfriends everywhere he went, even to funerals, Poulenc preferred to attend society affairs alone. He had always a strong sense of what was socially acceptable, and revelled in gossiping about his private life, as if divulging naughty secrets.

Composing out of a sense of duty never brought Poulenc his best results. He persisted in writing against the grain, perhaps because colleagues like Milhaud and Hindemith wrote in every conceivable form; Poulenc may have thought that a serious composer with ambitions to greatness was obliged to do likewise. Another unsatisfying work from 1948, *Quatre Petites Prières de Saint François d'Assise* did not suffer from blandness, but its basic problem was similar. The work was hampered by the fact that Poulenc respected St Francis, but was really more fond of St Anthony of Padua; Francis of Assisi tended to intimidate the composer. The idea for the work had not come from Poulenc himself, but from his great-nephew Roger, who was a monk at Champfleury. The opening hymn to the Virgin Mary has some strong Verdian harmonies, followed by formal, stately praise of 'Almighty God'. Poulenc's first error may have been to set St Francis's hymns in French, as the words are drab in French translation. The result is dutiful but not inspired. The final prayer says that 'pleasure is short, pain is eternal', and it is hard to imagine a composer less suited than Poulenc to set hellfire messages. Even when the subject matter of the work is somewhat inappropriate and even when conducted with sympathy, as by Robert Shaw, it is not entirely convincing.

In November 1948 Poulenc made his first tour of the USA with Pierre Bernac, supported by the baritone Doda Conrad, Marya Freund's son and a singer with Nadia Boulanger's group. The American experience was a revelation for Poulenc, and not just because, as he crowed to a friend, he had seduced a young clergyman in Boston. Musically, the trip resulted in numerous commissions, including a piano concerto for the Boston Symphony Orchestra. Most of all, he announced, at last he had found a place where he felt loved.

Unfortunately, Poulenc's Piano Concerto continued the composer's roll of disappointing compositions. It was dedicated to Denise Duval and Raymond Destouches, towards whom, after their sexual relationship of several years, Poulenc now felt only fatherly sentiments. Poulenc followed the tradition of the foreign virtuoso pianist–composer arriving with his new composition, as Sergey Rachmaninov had done in 1909, when he gave the première of his Third Piano Concerto on an American tour. Although Poulenc despised Rachmaninov, his Piano Concerto opens with a bow to that composer's Third Piano Concerto. Poulenc was a Russophile who idolized Mussorgsky and Stravinsky, and when performing his concerto, he clothed himself as a Russian, rather as he had dressed up as Landowska at Noizay.

The Concerto is in three movements, Allegretto commodo, Andante con moto and Rondo à la française (presto giocoso). The second movement begins poetically in the rhythm of a heartbeat. The final movement, however, is in the popular Nogent-style which Poulenc had made his own thirty years before. In this Concerto, the piano collaborates with the orchestra, rather than playing an adversarial role. Although this approach worked for Maurice Ravel in his piano concertos, it seemed ill-focused in Poulenc's work. Poulenc's longtime enemy, the Swiss critic R. Aloys Mooser, hated the Concerto's 'indigence of harmonic treatment whose deliberate and lazy platitude is worthy of a house of ill fame'. A review in *Le Figaro* of July 1950 was slightly more enthused: 'Certainly it isn't a concerto at all, but a little picture of manners, done up by a minor master.' Defenders explain the Concerto as an example of deliberate 'aesthetic discontinuity'; less indulgent listeners might decide that in this work the composer mastered orchestration, but content and form continued to puzzle him. Perhaps Poulenc had really wanted to compose another ballet-with-piano, such as *Aubade*. The merry Finale of the Concerto, which shocked some audiences by its lightness, was at least dynamic. But the twists and turns throughout the Concerto seem at times like random leaps from one idea to the next. The pianos of Poulenc's Concerto for two pianos discuss matters with a lively and amusing back-and-forth, whereas the solo instrument of the later concerto appears to be in a friendly wonderland, where anything goes.

An appearance of self-indulgence fuelled diatribes by critics such as Emile Vuillermoz, who published a *Histoire de la musique* (1949), in which he described Poulenc's production as being that of a 'courtly abbé', an oozy, flattering, socialite clergyman, a characterization which Poulenc spent most of his life trying to live down. Critics, who hardly knew Poulenc, would tend to read his music in the light of his social personality. True, Poulenc could be an ingratiating flatterer: he told Stravinsky that he wept to think he would miss the new ballet *Orphée*, 'every measure of which I love'. But a couple of days later he told a friend that he disliked *Orphée*, because it was 'more willed than inspired, and a little forced in its grandeur'.

Poulenc was in a slump which was hard to explain. Having written virtual masterpieces in *Les Mamelles de Tirésias* and *Figure humaine*, he may have been at a loss as to how to surpass himself. His generally declining physical condition may also have been a factor, for someone whose preferred nocturnal prowl was searching among Parisian pissoirs for sexual adventure. At fifty, Poulenc accepted the intricacies of his own personality. This complexity, however, still seemed to

Pierre Bernac's vague resemblance to Paul Eluard – high forehead, prominent nose and ears – may have played a role in Poulenc's affectionate trust in the poet. Bernac's gentlemanliness was a rare treasure in the music world.

The monumental painting *La Danse* by Henri Matisse (1869–1954): his art particularly inspired Poulenc, who believed that he wrote some songs by a method similar to that of Matisse, starting with a complex image and paring it down to a few essential lines.

puzzle his friends and listeners. In a July 1950 article in *Paris-Presse*, his friend Claude Rostand coined the term that would often be used to describe Poulenc: 'le moine et le voyou' (half monk, half thug). Although the phrase was intended to describe an audible diversity in the composer's work, the result was to suggest a sort of schizophrenia, or lack of control, which made Poulenc seem less than a serious creator. Christian Dior at least honoured the composer in his winter collection of 1950, in which the gowns were named after composers: Schubert, Mozart, Francis Poulenc ... Yet at this time, even when Poulenc focused on surefire material for his music such as the poems of Eluard, the results were less satisfying than before.

A new song setting to Eluard's poems, *La Fraîcheur et le Feu* had its première in November 1950. Poulenc considered this work to be a single poem cut into pieces and set to music, because the seven short poems of which it is comprised are highly fragmented and interdependent. Poulenc structured his work in alternating slow and fast tempos -'la fraîcheur' and 'le feu' respectively: 'Rayon des yeux', 'Le matin les branches attisent', 'Tout disparut', 'Dans les ténèbres du jardin', 'Unis la fraîcheur et le feu', 'Homme au sourire tendre', and 'La grande rivière qui va'. The composer claimed to be have been much influenced by the art of Matisse in writing this cycle, both in its clarity and simplicity, but also in its continuity of vocal line, without development or variations. More generally speaking, Matisse represented for Poulenc the example of an artist who toiled mightily to achieve results that appeared effortlessly simple and beautiful – and *La Fraîcheur et le Feu* is one of Poulenc's most seamlessly structured groups of songs. Poulenc achieved symmetry by ending the final song with the same music that began the first; he stressed the necessity of assembling the machine precisely, so that at the time of performing the work it would be possible to forget everything and seem to be improvising instinctively.

La Fraîcheur et le Feu was dedicated to Stravinsky and one of the songs, 'Tout disparut', marked 'very calm', quotes a melody from Stravinsky's piano *Sérénade en la.* In the title song of the cycle, Poulenc took the poet's exhortations personally: 'Unite coolness and fire … unite lips and eyes … expect wisdom from your madness … Make images of women and men.' Poulenc chose a poem – the 'Unis la Fraîcheur et le Feu' – that admired both partners in a heterosexual couple, telling of 'Man with two useful hands … Woman with hands of reason …' He was often attracted to each member of a married couple individually, and also attracted to their togetherness as a couple. (He addressed Marie-Blanche and Jean de Polignac as 'Pretty Countess, Pretty Count'.) But the piano accompaniment to this song is stern, beginning and ending with lengthy silences.

After *La Fraîcheur et le Feu,* the composer wrote no more songs for four years. He escaped from the series of not entirely satisfying works with a large-scale religious composition, for the first time since his 1937 Mass. When his friend Christian Bérard died in 1949, Poulenc decided to write a work in his memory. A Requiem seemed too pompous and he decided upon a *Stabat Mater* instead, having mastered choral writing by producing choruses in *Sécheresses, Les Mamelles de Tirésias, Figure humaine* and other vocal works. The switch from his Concerto to the *Stabat Mater* posed no problems, as he wrote to a woman friend:

Opposite, Christian Bérard's designs for Jean Giraudoux' play *La Folle de Chaillot* were seen as a high-water mark of French stage décor. The mournfully tatty garb of a madwoman was transformed into poetry by Bérard's visual talent.

By the way, you know that I am as sincere in my faith, without any messianic screamings, as I am in my Parisian sexuality. The personality problem is never posed for me. My musical tone is spontaneous, and in any case, I think, truly personal.

Stabat Mater was written in the form of a 'grand motet' for a five-part choir in the old French style, perfected by such seventeenth-century composers as Jean-Baptiste Lully. The work has twelve movements, an apostolic number that was not accidental, and they alternate artfully between calm and impassioned tempos: 'Stabat mater dolorosa' (very calm); 'Cujus animam' (very slow); 'Quæ mœrebat' (Andantino); 'Quis est homo' (Allegro molto); 'Vidit suum' (Andante); 'Eja mater' (Allegro); 'Fac ut ardeat' (Maestoso); 'Sancta mater' (Moderato, then Allegretto); 'Fac ut portem' (Sarabande, slow); 'Inflammatus et accensus' (animated and very rhythmic); 'Quando corpus' (very calm). The orchestra is used discreetly and is often not present at all for choral passages, in which the writing shows an intimate collaboration and blending of voices in the male and female choruses. Poulenc would later say, with slight exaggeration, that *Stabat Mater* was a chorus *a cappella* while his future *Gloria* was a great choral symphony. The restraint gives the *Stabat* its dignity. To this Poulenc adds the vocal luxury of three solos for lyric soprano; this dichotomy between luxury and restraint was not just part of Poulenc's personality, but also a characteristic of his late friend Christian Bérard.

Bérard was a talented painter and stage designer for plays by Jean Giraudoux, such as *La Folle de Chaillot*. A prodigious worker, he was capable of truly poetic creations, often in collaboration with the legendary actor Louis Jouvet. Bérard was an obese man who bathed rarely and spent days in bed with his dog, eating and joking with friends. Welcome in the upper reaches of high society, he had a taste for transvestism in seedy Paris dives. Bérard's portraits, like the one of Poulenc painted in 1934, added softness to even the harshest features. His sudden death was considered an 'irreparable loss' by Cocteau.

Following page, Christian Bérard; when he died, even the steely-eyed Nancy Mitford was moved, commenting that at the funeral, Bérard's lover Boris Kochno was so crushed that for the first time he seemed sympathetic to her.

With Bérard, Poulenc buried another element of his joyous youth. But it was not only Bérard who was mourned in the work: *Stabat*

La Folle
de Chaillot
Bérard

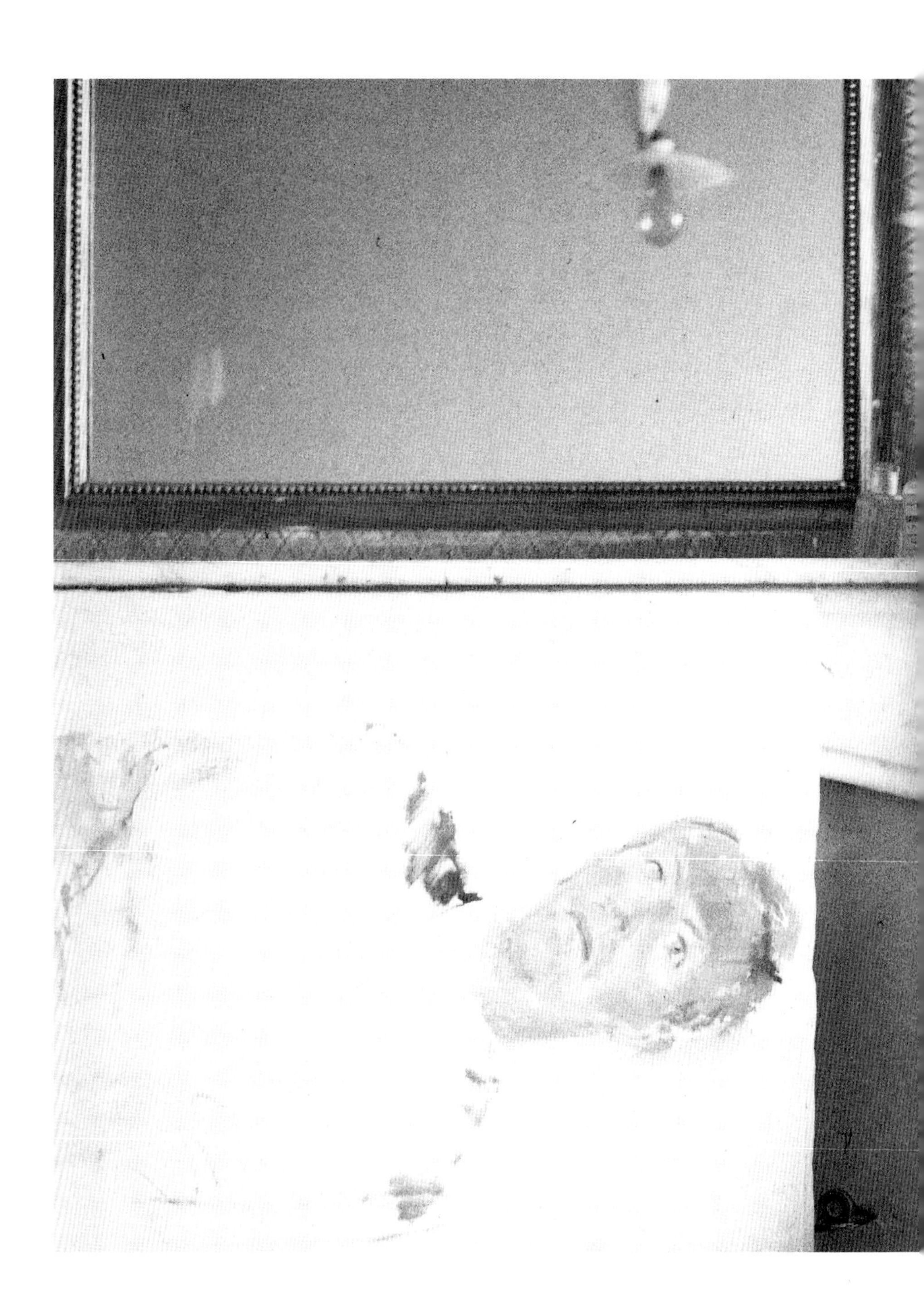

Mater depicts the Virgin Mary grieving over the suffering and death of her Son, a timely theme during the aftermath of World War II. The work is not exclusively despairing; in the final movements the listener can perceive a growing confidence. The tenth movement, 'May I bear the death of Christ', is written in a graceful sarabande, as if guiding the listener to sustain grief with poise. The Judgement Day is briefly evoked in the eleventh movement, far more convincingly than in the choral prayers of St Francis a few years before. In the twelfth and last movement, a plea for paradise after his own death, the composer offers the sensuous beauty of soprano and choir in late Romantic Italian style. A *forte* brass conclusion ends the work in a decisive manner.

Poulenc stressed the austere aspects of *Stabat Mater* and for the 1951 première he chose as conductor the stern Fritz Munch, brother of the ebullient conductor Charles Munch. After having studied to be a pastor, Fritz Munch headed the Strasbourg Conservatory and Institute of Musicology. He represented the pious rigour that Poulenc sought in the interpretation of his *Stabat*, not Charles Munch's 'half-drugged half-paradisical side'.

Poulenc was back on the right track. His next work, *Quatre Motets pour un temps de Noël* (1951–2), was one of his most gratifying. The *a cappella* motets for four-part chorus are highly visual, the product of a composer who has studied hundreds of religious paintings, and who tried to evoke some landscapes in his writing for voices. Of the four, 'O Magnum Mysterium' is the most performed, followed by 'Quem vidistis pastorem','Videntes stellam' and 'Hodie Christus natus est'. The writing for 'Videntes stellam' ('seeing the star') is especially magical, its high-reaching harmonies seeming to seek the star that the Magi saw in the sky. The pliant, sensitive vocal line has dramatic point: a rest after the word 'Magi' gives a solid image of the Three Kings, and underlines their stately importance. The words 'videntes stellam' are repeated numerous times, with a final cadence on a lower tone, as if the chorus brought the message to heart-level, absorbing the Nativity story into themselves. Bringing the story back to a human level by lowering the notes is subtle performing psychology, and only a composer deeply familiar with choral singing and composing would have thought of it.

The American duo pianists Arthur Gold and Robert Fizdale charmed Poulenc with both their musical talent and their homosexuality.

Poulenc continued in good form for a new commission, a Sonata for two pianos for the American pianists Arthur Gold and Robert Fizdale, a technically adroit duo who played with considerable aplomb. Young, handsome, and quite evidently a homosexual couple, they were introduced to Poulenc during an American tour, and were adopted by Poulenc and his circle of French friends as 'the Kiddies'. Although fleet and smart, Gold and Fizdale sometimes lacked the

Le groupe des Six n'a été qu'un groupe de six amis dont le seul plaisir était de se rejoindre et de travailler ensemble. Il n'a jamais été une école mais un mouvement. C'est pourquoi je suis fier d'avoir toujours été son porte parole.

Jean Cocteau
1951

By 1951, when Jean Cocteau scribbled this reminiscence about Les Six, much had intervened to separate the musical group of the 1920s, physically as well as artistically.

theatricality needed for performing Poulenc's piano works. His Sonata for two pianos (1952–3) was an ambitious document of inner emotions, which had little to do with the merry young Americans who commissioned it. With four movements, Prologue, Allegro molto, Andante lyrico and Epilogue, it was three times as long as the 1918 Sonata for piano duet and vastly more accomplished. Poulenc described at length the new work's structure, as if justifying his musical architecture. According to him, the Prologue was not like the first movement of a classical sonata, but a foreshadowing of the rest of the work, containing an extremely slow central theme of lyric importance. It was in the mode of Debussy's *La Cathédrâle engloutie*, with a measured, inevitable progression of fate. The Allegro molto is a scherzo, whose most important feature was an 'extraordinarily peaceful' central section. The fast sections are never carefree and, like the first movement, the second movement Allegro ends in tragic monumentality.

The composer considered the Andante the focus of the work, unlike the Andante of his Concerto for Two Pianos, which he admitted was mainly an imitation of Mozart; here Poulenc strove for profound lyricism and *élan*, with monumental writing in the Mussorgsky tradition. He drew inspiration from his choral compositions for the harmonic voices of the Andante, keeping an ideal of linear purity in mind. Poulenc enjoyed playing orchestral scores with friends in two-piano versions, and parts of the Sonata for two pianos sound like an orchestral reduction, where one piano plays the orchestra part and the other takes the soloist's role. Poulenc was particularly proud of the bass notes played in unison at the end of the Andante. The Epilogue was not intended as a finale, but rather as a recapitulation of the other three movements. It interweaves tunes of Nogent-style dynamism with heavy funeral marches. The mood is Lisztian gloom, highly pianistic and at the same time bearish; in its jaunty glee that also contains morbid forebodings it has similarities to the musical portrait of Max Jacob in *Le Bal masqué*. Although the composer never specified it, the Epilogue to his Sonata for two pianos may be a sort of requiem for Jacob.

Unlike his joyous Concerto for Two Pianos, the Sonata for two pianos offered 'the gravity of a string quartet', according to Poulenc.

Following page, On with the lunettes! In this 1950s reunion photo of Les Six all of the group are wearing glasses, even Cocteau and Honegger who were usually too vain ever to be photographed wearing spectacles.

The work is massive and tragic, and was clearly composed by someone who had known discouragement. Despite its sombre air, Poulenc's work was lyrical and accessible, unlike Pierre Boulez's *Structures*, another French work written for two pianos in 1951–2. Because of its technical and emotional difficulty, the Sonata for two pianos is not often heard. Duo-pianists find it more gratifying to perform *L'Embarquement pour Cythère, valse-musette* (1951), an appealing trifle which makes a charming encore. It is one of the composer's most-recorded pieces and has encouraged the image of Poulenc as a lightweight. One of Poulenc's instructions to the pianists was to play a section of *L'Embarquement* 'thickly, like a bloke's kiss, in a steady tempo'.

The sombre preoccupations of the Sonata for two pianos and *Stabat Mater* were a clue that in his next work Poulenc would be focused on meditative and religious subjects. This time, instead of another orchestral work with choir, Poulenc would return to the domain of opera.

7

Dialogues des Carmélites 1953–6

Poulenc's masterpiece, the opera *Dialogues des Carmélites*, proved that he saw no contradiction between his ardent Catholic piety and his hyperactive gay sex life. (Sopranos Elsie Morison and Jeanette Sinclair in the 1958 Covent Garden production)

I bought the book [Dialogues des Carmélites] *and decided to reread it. For that, I sat down at the outdoors café Tre Scalini on the Piazza Navone. It was ten in the morning. At noon I was still there, having consumed a coffee, an ice cream, an orange juice, and a bottle of Fuggi mineral water to justify my prolonged presence. At twelve-thirty I was drunk with enthusiasm but the final question remained – would I find the music for such a text? I opened by chance the book and forced myself instantly to translate into music the first sentences I read ... As incredible as it may seem, I immediately found the melodic line. Destiny had decided.*

Francis Poulenc, *Moi et mes amis*

Dialogues des Carmélites 1953–6

In the spring of 1950 a random encounter greatly influenced Poulenc's production during the decade: in a train he met a travelling salesman, Lucien Roubert, who had been born in Toulon (in 1908) but was then living in Marseilles. They embarked on a stormy relationship and when Poulenc was not composing, Lucien took up a good deal of his time, as a source of both physical pleasure and spiritual pain. Poulenc stated that just as Raymond Destouches had been the secret of *Mamelles* and *Figure humaine*, Lucien was that of *Stabat* and the *Carmélites*. Alternating between emotionally charged visits to Lucien and the solitude of work at Noizay, Poulenc told the bass Doda Conrad, 'How lucky you are to roll in the fine sand with a young American pianist. I live solitary, virtuous, and bent over myself (this posture does not imply onanism, I beg to reassure you).' However, he could not always joke about living far from his beloved. To some, his passion for a travelling salesman may have appeared less than serious, but Poulenc, who had an insatiable appetite for being loved, explained that his life till then had lacked sweetness, and now that fine feelings were involved, distance was a problem. Love was also his priority in musical matters and he instructed listeners not to criticize his music, but to love it. He was not, however, prepared to adopt such indiscriminate feelings towards other composers, such as Fauré, who he admired without loving, and Bach, for whom he felt 'indifferent adulation'. On tour in Caracas, Venezuela, Poulenc became fascinated, though not in love 'in the bad sense of the term', with the 'very handsome' forty-year-old conductor Sergiu Celibidache with whom he was playing the *Concert Champêtre*.

Despite his appetite for love, Poulenc did not foresee that his relationship with Lucien Roubert might take a tragic turn. He now felt paternal affection for the twice-married Raymond Destouches, who he called 'my old bristly fox'. Although their relationship was no longer sexual, it still occupied his emotional energy. In addition to this, his demanding young lover, Lucien, was expecting total dedication. Poulenc, suffering from eyestrain and other ailments linked to overwork and high living, complained that Lucien's overemphatic love terrified him. It may have been that after years of random, semi-public sexual encounters, he was distressed by the notion of a restrictive 'marriage' with another man.

Amid this emotional maelstrom, in the summer of 1952, the Italian music publisher Ricordi contacted Poulenc with a commission to write a ballet for La Scala. The work would be conducted, after ten rehearsals, by the maestro Victor de Sabata. Ricordi suggested as a subject the life of a woman martyr saint, a notion that may have been inspired by the successful 1952 Paris revival of the Virgil Thomson and Gertrude Stein opera *Four Saints in Three Acts*. Poulenc toyed with idea of a ballet on Saint Ursula: 'Martyrdom often struck saints in civilian clothes, so there won't be any Carmélites dancing on their toes.' In 1953, on a concert tour to Italy with the cellist Pierre Fournier, Poulenc spoke with Ricordi's director, Guido Valcarenghi. He confessed that he was not interested in writing a ballet about Saint Margarita of Cortona, as Ricordi had suggested, but preferred to create an opera, preferably on a mystical subject. Valcarenghi suggested *Dialogues des Carmélites*, a screenplay about Carmélite nuns beheaded during the French Revolutionary era, written by Georges Bernanos, the Catholic writer best known for his novel, *Journal d'un curé de campagne*. Bernanos usually dealt with Catholic themes in an ornate prose style, but *Dialogues des Carmélites* was atypical, and, having been sketched out for treatment as a film, the words were more pared-down than usual. They tell the story of Blanche de la Force, a novice in a group of Carmélite nuns at Compiègne, who is guillotined after she elects to be a martyr. Blanche goes calmly to her fate, unlike a First Prioress, who is shown dying of old age in distress and moral disarray. Poulenc had seen the play twice in Paris and reread it at home, but had never thought of it as a possible opera. Examining a copy for its prosody, he realized that the project was meant for him and so cabled his acceptance to Ricordi.

Poulenc was ripe to write a major work. He was bidding against his contemporaries such as Milhaud and Honegger for the position of greatest French composer. In April 1953 in Monte Carlo, there was a two-day festival of Poulenc's music, including symphonic works like *Sinfonietta*, the Piano Concerto, *Aubade* and *Les Biches*. The honours continued: he was named Officier de la Légion d'honneur in October 1953 and was presented with his decoration by the novelist Colette at her apartment in the Palais Royal. Later he commented, 'I feel like an old gentleman since they gave me the decoration. I may be exaggerating, but it seems to me I have fewer erections since!!!' He had just written a series of radio interviews with the journalist Claude Rostand, which would be published in book form, and had prepared another series of interviews with a close friend, Stéphane Audel, which also appeared in book form some years later. Poulenc used these books to re-establish ties with friends who had drifted away. Published flattery evoked friendly responses from Honegger, Durey and Henri Sauguet.

Poulenc knew that his opera would first be staged in Italian at La Scala. To prepare, he immersed himself in the world of Italian opera. Following Bernac's advice, he examined the Verdi roles of Amneris in *Aida* and Azucena in *Il trovatore* to learn about the vocal possibilites of an Italian contralto, which was useful for writing the role of the First Prioress. As Poulenc began work on the new opera, EMI France decided to record *Les Mamelles de Tirésias*, in response to a demand from America, without inviting the composer to the recording sessions. The *Mamelles* record turned out to be one of the great joys of Poulenc's life, and he wept with emotion on hearing it. These encouragements affirmed his choice of an opera project. Poulenc carefully studied Malipiero's 1929 edition of Monteverdi's *Orfeo*, which, although historically inaccurate, offered precious insights into word-setting and vocal lines.

Writing *Carmélites* proved emotionally taxing because 'one is always on the heights', and Poulenc identified his shaken emotions, due to his relationship with Lucien Roubert, with his progress. The physical separation from Lucien seriously unsettled the composer, who no longer had the reassuring presence of Raymond Destouches in his home. (Raymond had moved out of the composer's home to a nearby house with his new bride. Poulenc told friends how he missed 'the shared bathroom, after twenty years of habit'.) What Poulenc later diagnosed as male menopause was at the time frighteningly real.

Opposite, The British homosexual couple,Peter Pears, left, and Benjamin Britten, right, here shown with Poulenc at Cannes in 1954, were ardent performers of Poulenc's vocal works; their recordings are however buried in BBC archives, inaccessible to music lovers.

Always a hypochondriac, in 1954 Poulenc developed a paranoid certainty that he had stomach cancer. This was proved false by medical tests, but Poulenc's panic was unabated and he rationalized that this climate of anguish was necessary for the *Carmélites.*

Minor annoyances included the failure of the Paris Conservatoire to appoint Pierre Bernac to a teaching post, due to the Paris education system's cabal of self-protecting mediocrities. This meant that Bernac would not be able to retire from singing immediately and would continue to tour with Poulenc until he was sixty. Their next trip was to Egypt, against the will of Poulenc, who hated exotic travel. Poulenc finished the first Act of the *Carmélites* in Alexandria, but was depressed by tombs and funerary art, which reminded him of tombstone vendors at Père Lachaise: 'This art uniquely based on death depresses and bores me. I often feel like biting an Egyptologist (they're usually quite ugly!!!).'

Haunted by Egyptian images of death, his cancerophobia and his relationship with Lucien, Poulenc soon had another problem, involving the stage rights to the *Carmélites.* Bernanos's heirs approved Poulenc's idea to adapt the work, but they were not in a position to decide. Bernanos had written the work for a film based on a novel, *The Last to the Scaffold,* by a German writer, Gertrud von le Fort, and the adaptation rights to this book had been bought by an American screenwriter, Emmet Lavery. The Bernanos family disliked Lavery intensely, but, nevertheless, it was he who controlled the rights to the *Carmélites.* After months of negotiation, Lavery agreed to let Poulenc stage his opera on condition that his name appear on every programme and on the printed score. Poulenc had no choice but to agree. Thus his name is associated for eternity with that of Lavery, author of *The First Legion: a Drama of the Society of Jesus* (1934) and *Murder in the Nunnery* (1944).

Father Griffin, a Carmelite priest from Dallas, wrote to Poulenc to inquire about the opera's progress. On receiving the composer's reply that God only knew if he would finish it, the priest promised that every Carmelite in the USA would say a novena for Poulenc so that he might complete the work. This novena amused and inspired Poulenc, but did not prevent him from going through 'six weeks of anxious near-madness', which finally resulted in neurological treatment.

For a good part of 1954 Poulenc was stuck in the middle of his second act, without knowing if his opera would be staged, whether he had cancer, or if he could survive separation from a man he loved. In the autumn of 1954, after considerable treatment, Poulenc set off on a recital tour to Holland with Bernac. He presented new songs from two of his favourite poets: two by Max Jacob, grouped under the title *Parisiana*, and 'Rosemonde' by Guillaume Apollinaire. These three songs were the only other music Poulenc produced during the years he devoted to the *Carmélites*. The first of the Max Jacob songs, 'Joueur du bugle', had been cut from *Le Bal masqué* and retained that work's bizarre and unsettling evocation of Nogent, in a slow and unyielding tempo, as the composer instructed the pianist: 'sweetly punctuated, but with lots of pedal'. By contrast, the second song, 'Vous n'écrivez plus?', has the melodic lightness and drollness of Offenbach. However, the title voiced Poulenc's constant anxiety, that Lucien was not writing to him often enough. The Apollinaire song, 'Rosemonde', was a tender ode to transitory sex. The narrator sings of a girl he spent two hours with in Amsterdam, before leaving to seek the 'Rose of the World'. Casual sex as a road to the Holy Grail preoccupied Poulenc throughout his life; meeting Lucien in a train turned into one of the love stories of his life and Raymond had also been met by chance. In his high-society circle of friends, Poulenc was unlikely to be formally introduced to the lower-class men with whom he found happiness, so he was forced to seize any opportunity that might arise from impromptu meetings. 'Rosemonde' suggests that such chance encounters could be controlled by a spiritual, almost divine, religious power. Both for its philosophy and and for its gentle melody, 'Rosemonde' ranks among the composer's outstanding songs.

Although he managed to produce fine music, his emotional state steadily worsened. In the autumn he claimed not to have laughed since April, because he could not be happy with Lucien or without him. He took so many sedatives that he called himself 'a musical spectre', and began to wonder whether the *Carmélites* project was a cause, as if 'these terrible ladies', before losing their heads, wanted him to sacrifice his own as well. Poulenc complained continually about his woes, until the exasperated Bernac accused him of lacking 'moral virility' and of exhausting the affections of the 'loyal but uninteresting'

Although the stage director Margarita Wallmann (here rehearsing the 1958 Covent Garden production of *Carmélites*) made important contributions to the La Scala première, Poulenc referred to her as a 'Viennese Jewess' and had her replaced for the Paris production.

Lucien. He was not sure that Poulenc really loved Lucien as much as he claimed; following a quarrel with the younger man, Poulenc had hurried to seek a new lover, but remained jealous of whoever Lucien might replace him with. Bernac wished that Poulenc would indeed find someone else, 'if having arrived at our age, you really haven't managed to find another formula for your old age.' He exhorted Poulenc to save the last shreds of his dignity and not go to pieces as if he were the first person ever to suffer for love. He reiterated the request that Poulenc act with dignified strength, threatening to cancel their forthcoming tour because he could no longer stand the strain of Poulenc's hysteria. They continued a planned tour to Germany in November 1954, but Poulenc had to be brought back to Paris and admitted to a clinic for a three-week insomnia cure. The year ended with Poulenc still awaiting official permission to go ahead with his opera. He was now utterly reliant on barbiturates in order to get more than two hours' sleep a night and his mental state was weak: 'Black butterflies are still flying around me.' Yet music, whenever possible, was a saving grace.

He started off the New Year by playing his Concerto for Two Pianos with Britten at London's Royal Festival Hall on 16 January 1955 and he gave a recital with Bernac at Newcastle-Upon-Tyne on 20 January. Finally, permission to stage the *Carmélites* was granted and Poulenc had begun work when, in April, Lucien was struck by a deadly pleurisy. Responsible for Lucien's medical bills as well as his own, Poulenc insisted that Gold and Fizdale pay him the promised 1,000 dollars for the commission of the Sonata for two pianos. Lacking the cash, the pianists were bailed out by a rich American patron and amateur singer, Alice Esty. By July Poulenc hoped that Lucien was out of danger and in August he declared that his own menopause was over. Then Lucien took a turn for the worse with high fevers, and Poulenc was haunted by Bernanos's sentence in the *Carmélites*, 'We don't each die for ourselves, but some in the place of others.'

Francis and Lucien spent their last days together tranquilly. Lucien listened to the composer working at the piano and told him he had slept well for two hours, as Poulenc's funeral march had cradled him. One evening in October 1955, having finished copying out the

Carmélites, Poulenc told his maid that Lucien would die now that he had finished the opera: the same hour his prophecy was fulfilled. A six-year whirlwind relationship was over and Francis sought refuge at the home of Raymond Destouches, who never knew of Lucien's existence. Composing the *Carmélites* emptied Poulenc of religious feelings, and he felt as though he was in a spiritual desert. He was bored at Mass, and, having been so concerned for his own health, he was profoundly troubled by the idea that Lucien should have died instead of him.

Orchestrating the opera took the composer a good part of 1956. Each of the twelve scenes is dated by the year and place where it was written, such as Noizay, Paris, Lausanne, Cannes, Alexandria and Tourettes-sur-Loup, and in this litany of place-names, the musical score reads like the spiritual diary of a pilgrimage. When *Carmélites* is sung in Italian it exemplifies late Romantic vocal and orchestral traditions born in Italy, and, in this respect, it is a true Italian opera. Poulenc thanked Verdi in his dedication, but he might also have mentioned, among others, Puccini, Boito and Mascagni.

The opera follows the destiny of the heroine, Blanche de la Force, as she enters the cloister at Compiègne. Through a 'transfer of grace' she calmly elects to die with the other nuns, martyrs of the French Revolution. Humility and neurosis are central to the character of Blanche and when she is presented on stage in Act I, her vocal line is rapid and humble, like the servant Suzuki in Puccini's *Madama Butterfly*. Throughout the opera Poulenc used two themes repeatedly, which he insisted were not leitmotivs: Blanche's theme, taken from the Agnus Dei of his Mass (1937), and the First Prioress's theme, an agitated melody from the Organ Concerto. The orchestral accompaniment in Act I, when a servant explains how Blanche screamed in fright, is marked 'very slow, like a sleepwalker' and when she comes on stage after the First Prioress's death, the stage direction is 'enters, like a sleepwalker'. The unconscious world is very much a part of *Carmélites.*

Another name which could have been added to the dedication is that of Alban Berg, whose *Wozzeck* Poulenc admired. *Carmélites* is a synthesis of Romantic conventions with the psychological self-awareness of *Wozzeck*. Poulenc used his experiences with women to

Royal Opera House

COVENT GARDEN

HOUSE MANAGER . JOHN COLLINS

THE ROYAL OPERA HOUSE, COVENT GARDEN LIMITED

GENERAL ADMINISTRATOR . DAVID L. WEBSTER

in association with the Arts Council of Great Britain

presents

the first stage performance in Great Britain of

The Carmelites

(*"Dialogues des Carmélites"*)

Music by FRANCIS POULENC

Text of the drama by GEORGES BERNANOS

Adapted as an opera by permision of EMMET LAVERY:
the drama inspired by a novel of GERTRUDE VON LE FORT
and a scenario of REV. FR. BRUCKBERGER and PHILIPPE AGOSTINI

(Property of G. Ricordi & Co.)

CONDUCTOR — RAFAEL KUBELIK

PRODUCER — MARGHERITA WALLMANN

Scenery and costumes by WAKHEVITCH

Lighting by JOHN SULLIVAN

This opera has been realised by permission of M. Emmet Lavery, author of the official theatrical adaption of "Die Letzte am Schaffott" under the title "Song at the Scaffold" and joint owner with Mme. Gertrude von Le Fort of the copyright of the novel.

on

THURSDAY, 16th JANUARY, 1958

Opposite, the mention of both Emmett Lavery and Gertrud von le Fort on the first page of the Covent Garden programme for *Carmélites* reflects the anguished legal wrangles Poulenc endured in order to acquire the rights to have his work performed.

form his opera's psychological content and made all the characters live and breathe by basing them on complex, living models. He confessed that the wife of his friend Stéphane Audel, an actress in Louis Jouvet's troupe, was his model for Mère Marie; too bad she was unable to sing. Even the minor role of Sister Constance, a coloratura soprano, was beautifully detailed. In the first act Constance is manic, then depressive, announcing, 'At fifty-nine, isn't it really time to die?' (the composer was fifty-eight when he wrote these measures). Constance cries that serving God amuses her, with a high C on 'amuse' that recalls Ambroise Thomas's Titania in *Mignon*. A moment later she soberly announces that she always expected to die young and that people do not die for themselves, but for others, and even in the place of others.

In Act I, scene iv, the First Prioress dies in one of the great dramatic moments of modern opera. The emotional level is hysterical, as it must be for Italian opera, but musical dignity and refinement are

The Australian soprano Joan Sutherland (b. 1926) made a rare venture into modern music by performing in the 1958 Covent Garden staging of *Dialogues des Carmélites*, in the role of the Second Prioress.

British contralto Jean Watson made the most of the dramatic potential of the death scene of the First Prioress in the 1958 Covent Garden staging of *Dialogues des Carmélites*. Poulenc musically depicted death as an obscene horror, a macabre orgasm.

always present: such self-control, even at moments of acute tension, ranks Poulenc with modern opera composers like Luigi Dallapiccola. Mussorgsky was also a source, as the orchestra's bell-tolling before the death of the Prioress recalls the scene of Boris Godunov's madness and death. Poulenc told Bernac that the Prioress's death scene was 'very Amneris' in its passionate Verdi-style vocalizing in which raw emotion takes precedent over refinement, but she was also a deranged Azucena from *Il trovatore*. Her declaration that decades in the cloister do not help her at the end of her life, has the effect of portraying death as an obscenity. The Prioress's vocal part is marked in the score *très rude*, with such comments as 'we hear her death rattle', which, in performance, is a orgasmic moan with a cavernous ring. The other nuns in the convent are not convoked to bid farewell to the Prioress because she is not fit to be seen. Poulenc surpassed his predecessors in the Italian tradition in psychological acuity: the nuns are plausible women, earthy and primitive, or frivolous or neurotic.

The Second Prioress's long monologue in Act II shows off the dramatic soprano voice to its best advantage. The richness of vocal tone is part of bel-canto reassurance, although the ticking-clock motif returns from the scene of the First Prioress's death. The nuns sing an Ave Maria, not a spectacular showpiece, but like a humble prayer from an oratorio: the soloist's part is marked *dolcissimo* (and without crescendo) and the chorus sings with 'mouth closed, just a murmur'. Poulenc later commented, 'Who would have thought the angelic Ave Maria had been composed on a depressing day in January 1954 after Lucien stood me up!' He cherished a sense of freedom in asymmetry and indicated that the solo singers' voices on stage should be 'just a bit off, but very gently so' from the ensemble; he felt that pianists too should sometimes play with their hands not entirely together.

Another convention retained from romantic opera was the tenor-soprano love duet. A story of nuns' martyrdom does not lend itself to love duets, but Blanche's duo with her brother in Act II is definitely love music, without in the least evoking incest. The tenor is encouraged to open-throated Italianate singing, but with French refinement. When Blanche's brother speaks about her, his passages are marked 'with extreme tenderness' and 'softly'. Poulenc's stage instinct was right: at the La Scala première, the tenor-soprano duet won hearty applause, providing an outlet for the audience's pent-up tension from the anguish of the preceding scenes.

Without preaching or being didactic, the opera is very much a morality play. In Act III, scene ii, Mère Marie offered an aphorism that was central to Poulenc's experience as well as being applicable to any persecuted minority: 'The misfortune, my girl, is not to be despised, but only to despise oneself.'

Poulenc's opera was harmonious-sounding, which led some listeners to underestimate his ingenuity. At some dramatic moments, the sounds are fresh and new. Act III contains an interlude with

Following page, the scenes of Revolutionary France in *Dialogues des Carmélites*, in which talk is of the revolutionaries who merely 'howl with the wolves,' may have been Poulenc's indirect reference to French wartime collaborators.

spoken dialogue, accompanied by inventive percussion: a snare drum, tom-tom and wood block play in turns. This ensemble overlays the news of the inevitable event of the Carmelites' arrest with a sinister atmosphere, which evokes Asiatic torture. This interlude, with its knocking, tock-a-tock accompaniment, is a brilliant theatrical notion in which Poulenc may have hearkened back to the solo percussion movement of his youthful work *Jongleurs*. Interrupting the orchestra's flow catches the audience's attention and, when the orchestra resumes for the scene of beheadings, the public is gripped by the emotion of the event.

Despite Poulenc's previous acclaimed works, like *Stabat Mater*, *Un Soir de neige* and *Les Mamelles de Tirésias*, few listeners expected that *Carmélites* would be so good. Divine intervention may be one explanation for its success: Poulenc offered a silver chalice to the shrine of the Virgin of Rocamadour in 1957, as an action of grace for having finished the opera. In 1938 he had offered a silver ciborium to the same shrine after finishing *Litanies à la Vierge Noire* and both precious objects, made by the Parisian silversmith Puiforcat, formed the basis of the Musée-Trésor Francis Poulenc at the Rocamadour shrine.

The printed score of the opera is prefaced by a dedication to the memory of Poulenc's mother. He thanked Claude Debussy for giving him the taste to write music, and Claudio Monteverdi, Giuseppe Verdi and Modest Mussorgsky, who greatly influenced his opera. The epigraph was a quotation from Saint Theresa of Avila: 'God keep me from gloomy Saints.' In this elliptical dedication should be read the names of other composers who influenced the work, and perhaps above all one should read the name of the late Lucien Roubert. Poulenc was not prudish about dedicating a work to a male lover – he had already thanked Raymond in this way – but the nature of the subject may have inspired unusual restraint in this case.

Opposite, Blanche de la Force woth her brother Le Chevalier in Act I, scene i from the 1958 Covent Garden production of *Dialogues des Carmélites*

Following the religious experience of the *Carmélites*, Poulenc was more than ever attached to his worldly routine. From 1956 onwards he consoled himself with a new boyfriend, Claude, a 28-year-old junior executive at Citroën, and bragged to a friend from a luxury hotel at Evian:

It's rather remarkable, a maestro 57 years old, adored by a comfortable boy aged 28 who drives me around in his car, and invites me to good meals!!! I'm just about kept by him!!! I am profiting deliciously! But shhh, not a word to the Countess, or the Marquise, or the Duchess!!!

The world première of *Dialogues des Carmélites* took place at La Scala in Milan on 26 January 1957. Poulenc was present, although he had not been asked to help prepare the production. He had wanted his friend, the painter Jean Hugo, to design the sets, but Hugo claimed to be out of practice at stage design. Poulenc's suggestion that Denise Duval should sing the role of Blanche was refused by La Scala and the part was sung by Virginia Zeani, a young Romanian soprano specializing in bel canto. Gianna Pederzini (First Prioress), Leyla Gencer (Second Prioress), Giliola Frazzoni (Mère Marie), Eugenia Ratti (Sister Constance) and Scipio Colombo (Marquis de la Force) completed the cast; the conductor was Nino Sanzogno.

The reviews were vastly enthusiastic, especially from Parisian critics. *Le Monde* announced 'a great international event. A great French victory … We must return to such words as "grandeur, simplicity, nobility", ordinarily used in such mediocre ways, in order to understand all that is exceptional and rare in M. Francis Poulenc's creation.' *Le Figaro* stated that Poulenc's music

uses a harmonic language of such voluptuous richness that one might fear, at a first hearing, an excess of seduction. With such meaty chords, how could the musician have translated the mystery of self-denial? Yet Poulenc has carefully controlled his pen, and at the moment one thinks it is going to let go, he holds it back … It is quite clear that in Dialogues des Carmélites, *Poulenc has given us his masterpiece. And I do believe that it's a masterpiece in and of itself.*

Les Lettres françaises said that Poulenc 'knew how to remain himself while lifting himself to the heights. One may also admire the joyous vitality he accords to the novices in their daily life, as much as the Prioress's tragic death, the choruses including an ineffable Ave Maria, and the dramatic final scene where the musician attains the simplicity of a masterpiece.' Carpers were few: the March 1957 *Opera Magazine* called the work 'a considerable disappointment ... a score pervaded by monotony ... It is doubtful if it will outlive its initial attraction.'

Despite the success, Poulenc felt that the stage direction of Marguerite Wallmann had 'removed all emotion to the profit of decoration', claiming that she, 'as a Viennese Jewess, can only see things from the exterior'. In a letter to Milhaud, he more tactfully suggested that Wallmann was somewhat exterior to his opera 'because she comes from the ballet'. Although she was responsible for suggesting that *Dialogues des Carmélites* be in three acts instead of two as Poulenc had originally planned, Wallmann was replaced for the Paris production by a modest stage director, Maurice Jacquemont, who would not steal attention from the work. Poulenc gave a multitude of detailed suggestions to Jacquemont, whose name he misspelled in a number of letters: 'Act III, scene i – Arrange better the exit (fleeing) of Blanche. It shouldn't look like ... toilets.'

The Paris Opéra première of *Dialogues des Carmélites* on 21 June 1957 was a historic date. The cast included Denise Duval as Blanche de la Force, and Denise Scharley as the First Prioress; the conductor was Pierre Dervaux. Unlike at the La Scala première, Poulenc offered advice; this time the production tended towards a starker presentation visually and dramatically, and it was greeted with rapturous praise. The essayist Janet Flanner wrote in *The New Yorker* in 1957 that Poulenc's score was 'marked by his characteristic ecstasy of expression and subtlety of harmony, by lofty reaches of mounting melodic grace, by the rich polyphony of his chorales ... and by an all-too-brief last-act overture of really passionate loveliness.' There were a few dissenters, like the critic Frederick Goldbeck, who wrote: 'With a naïvety that requires cunning intelligence to maintain for so many years, Poulenc omits all heroism, and the least aesthetic audacity.' Yet he concluded,'Harmonically, musical archaism is the most characteristic element, both the main constituent of its style and the mainspring of its success.'

Opera houses worldwide tumbled over one another to perform the work. The New York Metropolitan Opera intended to stage *Dialogues des Carmélites* in 1958, but the San Francisco Opera outmanœuvred them by showing a production in September 1957,

The death of the Prioress, in the 1958 Covent Garden production of *Dialogues des Carmélites*; sets and costumes were by Georges Wakhevich, and the production was conducted by Rafael Kubelík, music director of Covent Garden (1955–8).

which starred Leontyne Price and was televised across the country. The frustrated director of the Metropolitan Opera, Rudolf Bing, decided never to stage *Dialogues des Carmélites* and its New York première was not until 1977, after his retirement. Otherwise, the opera had a smooth career. The Covent Garden première, sung in English on 16 January 1958, was conducted by Rafael Kubelik, with Elsie Morison as Blanche, Jean Watson (First Prioress); the cast also included Joan Sutherland and Sylvia Fisher. In Vienna, it was performed by Irmgard Seefried and other stars eleven times in 1958 and fourteen times in the 1959–60 season. Poulenc felt that although the Vienna production was perfect, it was cold, while at a production in Catania, 'There was inspired sperm in the air, if not underneath the costumes. Sicily resembled me more, but Vienna represented a rather assuring post-mortem glory.'

8

After the Carmelites 1957–63

Jokes with dear friends like Denise Duval helped Poulenc to forget temporarily his psychological agonies. Duval, one of Poulenc's favourite performers, retired from performing not long after Poulenc's death.

I leaf through this Journal with some melancholy. The time is no longer right for songs (at least for me). I have taken all that I *could from Eluard, Apollinaire, Max Jacob, etc. Our association with Bernac reaches its very end. I must look elsewhere.*

Francis Poulenc, *Journal de mes mélodies*

After the Carmelites 1957–63

In March 1957 Poulenc met another lover, Louis Gautier, a large, blond 29-year-old colonial infantryman. Relieved to have a physical relationship without being in love, he told a friend, 'It's been a long time since I've known such poetic moments, that's the word for it.' He joked, 'Nowadays it's more like *Dialogues with a Sergeant* instead of those ladies, but that's part of behind the scenes with creators ... You always need human compost to make lilies grow.' On his annual pilgrimage to the shrine at Rocamadour that year, Poulenc thanked the Virgin Mary 'for the *Carmélites*, and for meeting Louis (she understands everything).'

The relationship was a help rather than a hindrance to his composing career, and Poulenc referred to his new Flute Sonata as 'proof of the French Army's generosity on an old maestro's morale'. In response to the Elizabeth Sprague Coolidge Foundation in the USA, who had contacted him early in 1956 to request that he write a chamber work, Poulenc planned a Sonata for flute and piano. He postponed the delivery date, as he was busy orchestrating *Dialogues*, but in the summer of 1956 he felt free again, and dusted off a draft for a Flute Sonata that he had begun in 1952.

The Flute Sonata (for which his declared model was Debussy's formal writing) is in three movements, Allegro malinconico, Cantilena and Presto giocoso. In the opening movement the pianist was instructed to use lots of pedal, which he considered to be like 'putting butter in the sauce'. The middle Cantilena recalled the piano part of the song 'C', but the Finale had Nogent-style high spirits. There are also melodic reminiscences of *Dialogues des Carmélites* scattered through the Flute Sonata, which nevertheless retains an admirable lightness of tone. This music is lyricism for its own sake, with no literary programme, and it must have been a relief to compose this pure music, graceful for its own sake, without any textual associations.

The need to soar freely with melody was linked by the ageing composer to his romantic life. Today, few flautists do not wish to perform and record the Sonata, first played by the composer with flautist Jean-Pierre Rampal at the Strasbourg Festival in June 1957. At the première, the public was so enthusiastic that the performers had to repeat the second movement. *Le Figaro* compared the work's melodies to 'a great melodic rainbow with a background touched up with subtle blue harmonies'. The British composer Lennox Berkeley orchestrated the Flute Sonata, and although his skill was highly praised, the work is often considered to be lush enough in its chamber form.

In 1957 Poulenc also composed an *Elégie* for horn and piano, in memory of the great British horn player Dennis Brain (1921–57), who had died in a car crash. Poulenc was not a close friend of Brain's, although he may have met him through Britten or while recording for Walter Legge in London; but he knew Brain's poetic records, and may have wanted to write something for the talented horn player, as had Britten and Hindemith. The *Elégie*, in one movement of ten minutes, starts with striding impulses which are broken off abruptly, much as Brain's life was. This is mournful music, with elegant writing for the high range of the horn. The piece ends with a kind of blues feel, the muffled horn sounding at times like a saxophone, and the piano plays cadences to the chimes of Big Ben, as a tribute to Brain's nationality. The *Elégie* embraces the convention of death as cloud or fog, and England, as a foggy land, becomes by extension a land of death for young Dennis Brain.

England was the source of another musical request: Britten asked Poulenc to prepared a transcription for two pianos of *Les Mamelles de Tirésias*, for performance at the 1958 Aldeburgh Festival. Poulenc's resulting unpublished arrangement is appropriate for small-scale productions of *Mamelles.* The composer cancelled his trip to Aldeburgh at the last minute, forcing Britten to perform the arrangement with Viola Tunnard. Poulenc remained on cordial terms with Britten and Pears, who recorded his *Tel Jour, telle nuit* for the BBC, yet he did not care for much of Britten's music: he left after two acts of the 1952 Paris première of Britten's opera *Billy Budd.*

A commission from a rich American patron and amateur singer, Alice Esty, resulted in a new song cycle, *Le Travail du peintre.* She

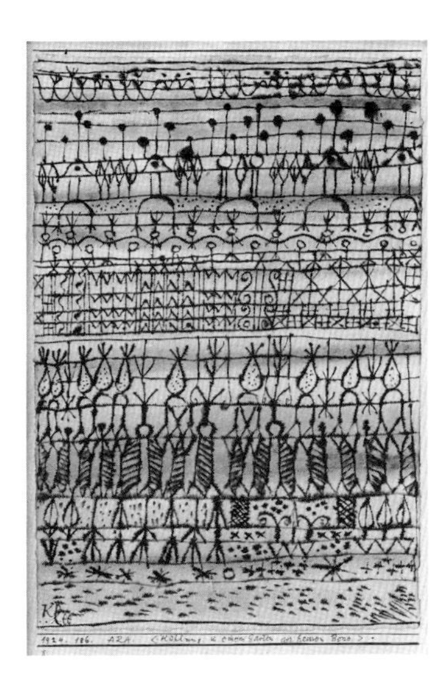

The works of (from top left, clockwise) Picasso, Klee, Gris, Miró, Villon, Braque and Chagall inspired Paul Eluard's collection, *Voir* (1948), which in turn inspired Poulenc's *Le Travail du peintre*.

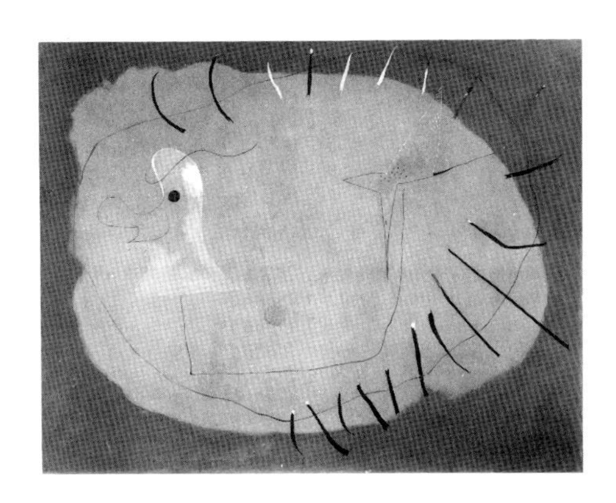

requested first performance rights for the cycle, which she planned to perform with her usual accompanist who, according to Bernac, played like a pig. Esty's vocal talents, Auric told Poulenc, '[did] not equal those she has for patronage'. Poulenc wanted the cash and behaved gallantly: 'How delicate it is to speak about money with a pretty woman!' He was tactful when Esty's accompanist sent him private recordings they had made of Poulenc songs. On 1 April 1957, Poulenc accompanied Esty in a Paris recital which included *Le Travail du peintre* and her usual pianist accompanied her in a variety of other songs. However, Bernac and Poulenc considered their own performance of the cycle on 5 September 1957 at the Edinburgh Festival as the world première.

The idea for *Le Travail du peintre* had been brewing for a while. In 1948 Eluard published a collection of poems, *Voir*, dedicated to painters, including Picasso, Chagall, Braque, Juan Gris, Paul Klee, Miró and Jacques Villon. Poulenc considered the poems for a song cycle, but wanted Eluard to write a poem about Matisse to end the work. However, Eluard did not share his admiration for Matisse, and when the poet died in 1952, the project had not advanced. By 1956 Poulenc believed that he had already said all that he could in the medium of song, but decided to write *Le Travail du peintre* as a posthumous tribute to Eluard. His songs primarily relate to the poems rather than to the painters, yet 'Pablo Picasso' is like its artistic model – granitic with a touch of Spanish cruelty. The melody is in C major, which recalls the opening of *Tel Jour, telle nuit*, but, as Poulenc observed, by this time the key of C major did not necessarily signify calm joy for him. 'Marc Chagall' is a scherzo, in the light Jewish vein of Poulenc's music in homage to Max Jacob. Poulenc had no special affinity for the work of Chagall, much preferring Dufy. As a devoted admirer of Picasso, Poulenc's rapport with Picasso's enemy Braque was ambiguous, and he later judged Braque's song as 'perhaps too tasteful, but that's how I feel about Braque'. More successful was 'Juan Gris' – Poulenc could empathize with Gris and his music added a dramatic commentary to the poet's description of a still-life. Of 'Paul Klee', Poulenc stated, 'I needed a *presto* here. It's a dry melody, which must clack.' The manic, surrealistic melody does not readily bring to mind Klee, whose art was more subdued and subtle than Poulenc's music would suggest.

'Joan Miró' also did not fully represent the artist in question. Marked *allegro giocoso*, its unfocused tune avoided the tragedy and nervousness in Miró's work. 'Jacques Villon', although its subject is perhaps the weakest artist of the group, is an artistic success; the composer adopted an air of farewell, producing a stern setting as he had done in Racine's 'Hymne'. Eluard's text explained that 'life is to be cherished, in spite of plagues', a sentiment with which Poulenc, having weathered many inner crises, agreed. He believed that this would be his last melody, and the strong sign-off matches the impressive opening of the cycle. Apart from 'Juan Gris', most of the songs are disappointing transition music and *Le Travail du peintre* must be rated as an uneven experiment in a valedictory tone, despite Poulenc's intention of 'renewing my songs by musically painting'.

Before Poulenc's farewell to songwriting was definitive, Doda Conrad asked him to write something in honour of his mother Marya Freund's eightieth birthday. Poulenc had accompanied Freund at a private concert of Satie's *Socrate* two years before; during preparations for the performance, Poulenc asked the 78-year-old Freund if she would like to sit down, to which the singer replied, 'One doesn't rehearse Satie's *Socrate* sitting down!' Recalling her performances of *Le Bestiaire* forty years earlier, Poulenc set another poem from Apollinaire's *Bestiaire*, 'La Souris'. It was another adieu, but this time a comic one. The song announced, 'I'm going to be 28...', charming when written by a 58-year-old composer, for an 80-year-old singer.

Fatigue and old age did not impede a few more last attempts at songwriting. A friend sent Poulenc a poem, 'Nuage' by the obscure Marseille poet Laurence de Beylie. No author's name was indicated on the typescript, but Poulenc liked the Maeterlinck-style impressionism of the poem. His setting ended with the declaration, 'all is written', as grave as the bass Arkel in Debussy's *Pelléas et Mélisande*.

Poulenc's valedictory air turned lugubrious in another song, 'Dernier Poème', by Robert Desnos (1900–45), the surrealist poet who died in a concentration camp. Poulenc identified with the message of love for a departed one, and exhaustion in the antechamber to death: 'I've walked so much, talked so much ... loved your shadow so much ... That I have nothing left of you ... I must be a shadow among shadows ...' Unfortunately, the vocal line is an overstated whine that does not do justice to the themes involved. The final song efforts of one of the century's best song composers were minor: an Eluard setting, 'Une chanson de porcelaine', for the eightieth birthday of the singer Jane Bathori, and his only English setting, Shakespeare's 'Fancy' (1962) from *The Merchant of Venice*, for a book of children songs to which Britten and Zoltán Kodály also contributed.

As *Dialogues* continued a triumphal march around the world, Poulenc was urged to try other opera projects. He thought of setting a realistic George Simenon-style story, or a Parisian theme like Marcel Carné's film, *Hôtel du Nord*, but abandoned these ideas, as he had his earlier plans to set an unpublished play by Apollinaire on Casanova. Hervé Dugardin, of the Paris Ricordi office, suggested that he turn Cocteau's monologue *La Voix humaine* into a short solo opera for Maria Callas. But 'La divina' resisted singing in languages other than Italian, and Poulenc was in any case more excited by the voice of Renata Tebaldi, Callas's arch-rival. When Poulenc finally took up Dugardin's idea, it was for Denise Duval.

Cocteau's play (1932) was about a young and attractive woman who has been discarded by her lover. She tries to keep him on the telephone by various ploys and eventually confesses that she tried to kill herself with pills the night before. Finally the conversation breaks off, and it is clear that that the woman, known only as 'Elle', has been abandoned for good.

One of Cocteau's dramatic ploys, the phone cutting off without warning, was an outdated device even when the play was first performed at the Comédie-française. But the cutting-off of phone conversations does divide the opera into natural sections.

Schoenberg had written an opera for one singer, *Erwartung*; Poulenc's aesthetic was more lyrical than expressionist, closer to Monteverdi's *Arianna abandonnata*, a Baroque lament for soprano. Poulenc wrote his opera without arias, and indeed, one of the only catchy tunes occurs at Elle's description of her suicide attempt, where the orchestra plays what Poulenc called a 'Sibelius-style *Valse triste* rhythm'. *La Voix humaine* follows the text's prosody so closely that it can seem musically disjointed. Poulenc regarded the soprano singing Elle as almost a co-composer of the role, in so far as she would decide when to take pauses; her music was taken at a free tempo, agreed upon with the conductor before the performance. Emotional flexibility was essential in order to change the mood rapidly from anxiety to calm. At the same time, Poulenc sought a sensual orchestral sound to bathe the onstage action.

A lot of nonsense has been suggested that because Cocteau and Poulenc were gay, the play and opera were really about an older man being dumped by his boy lover; Elle was obviously intended to be a credible woman, not Cocteau or Poulenc in drag. Nevertheless, the authors of *La Voix humaine* identified with Elle's situation. Many themes of Cocteau's play, the pills, the dread spectre of suicide and the love for a dog, were present in Poulenc's life, even if he were not living through the kind of rejection Elle experienced. A confirmed dog lover, Poulenc was devastated when his wire-haired terrier Mickey, nicknamed Toutou, died, and he inserted a sentimental moment in the opera when Elle speaks about her dog. Denise Duval complained that the audience's attention slackened and asked that the dog be cut from the opera in performance; Poulenc accepted, but insisted on reinstating it when the opera was recorded.

Both Poulenc and Cocteau were passionate observers of women. Poulenc, writing the opera for Duval, knew the details of the soprano's stormy love life, and this helped to cultivate a sense of specificity in the opera. With a painstaking eye for detail, Cocteau told Poulenc to take Duval to Alexandre's hairdressing salon on the rue du faubourg St-Honoré to get a hair attachment made, specifying that the wig should be tinted auburn, and neglected, as though she had not had it done for a few days. Although the title, *La Voix humaine* is sometimes taken in a grandiose way as representing all humanity, it was meant in a specific sense: Elle explains that when a person is reduced by the telephone to only 'a human voice', any cruelty is possible.

Poulenc poured immense anguish into his opera. He was revelling in the comfort of Louis's company, and not suffering from unrequited love; but he shared an emotional disarray with Elle. Like her he abused sleeping pills, tranquillizers and anti-depressants. He tried a stimulant, but it caused 'too much euphoria', and overmedicated, he claimed to be a 'sleepwalker' saluting crowds 'like an automaton'. With the medications Poulenc felt as though he were drying up as a composer. Poulenc's nerves were fragile and *La Voix humaine* reasserted his involvement in life and love. Being in love was not a good thing for Poulenc, but creating a plausible love situation on stage showed that he was still alive. More than ever he confided in letters to friends intimate details of his sex life.

He described the composition of *La Voix* to Hervé Dugardin of Ricordi editions:

It's a secret, but I've found all my themes. Two are incredibly erotic ... They smell of sperm, of between the thighs ... Blanche was me, and Elle is me again, and Louis, by anticipation. Life will necessarily take him from me in one way or another, that angel. He is exquisite to me and is a tender, polite, and deferential son (except at certain moments!).

Poulenc's fear of losing Louis was useful for attaining the hysterical atmosphere of *La Voix*, but the anguish was ill-founded – Louis remained loyal to him until the end of his life. Nevertheless, when work temporarily called Louis away from Poulenc's side, the elderly and insecure composer would feel the torments of abandonment. Poulenc suffered from increasing self-doubt and a lack of religious certainty; at insecure times, he would indulge in anti-Semitic remarks, such as when he wrote to Bernac: 'Cannes, which should be spelled Kahn, is odious.' Some relief was provided in July 1958, when he was named Doctor *honoris causa* at Oxford University. On 7 August he finished *La Voix humaine*, noting that the number seven was important for him because he was born on the seventh of the month. The Paris Opéra-Comique première of *La Voix humaine* in February 1959 was conducted by Georges Prêtre. Duval's intensity was such that after the second performance the orchestra gave her a standing ovation, a rare event in opera history.

At the beginning of 1959 Poulenc claimed to be broke, because Louis's projects for starting a small business and building a house had cost him dearly: 'I must accept commissions, although I have so little musical appetite. That's what love has reduced me to. In any case, I owe (Louis) *La Voix humaine*, that's something.' In March, Poulenc was almost suicidal, but he rationalized: 'My music alone restrains me. Operas by suicides are not performed.' He put on a courageous face in a live television concert in May 1959, accompanying Jean-Pierre

Rampal and Denise Duval. He also performed in a concert celebrating his sixtieth birthday on 27 May; this was the last time Pierre Bernac, also aged sixty, sang in public.

Poulenc toyed with the idea of another opera of a Cocteau play, *La Machine infernale*, to no avail. An *Elégie* for two pianos was written at the request of Gold and Fizdale in memory of Poulenc's friend Marie-Blanche de Polignac, who had died in 1958. Not at all mournful, the work was 'very Chabrier', according to the composer, who instructed performers to play it as if 'improvising, a cigar between your lips and a glass of cognac on the piano'. One Chabrier aspect was the musical parody of 'Home on the Range' which begins this work, written as a token of friendship for the American piano duo. The jokes were a fond recollection of de Polignac's parties at her Brittany estate, Kerbastic, where Poulenc amused himself so much that he forgot his strong dislike of Brittany. But this *Elégie* for two pianos (1959) has nowhere near the musical or emotional interest of the *Elégie* for horn and piano of a couple of years before, and it was his last composition for piano: Poulenc was clearly treading water.

Even the challenge of a large new commission did not stir him from his lethargy. The Koussevitsky Foundation of Boston asked for a new symphony, but Poulenc told them that he was not interested in writing one, and when they countered by asking for an organ concerto, he replied that he had already written one. Finally, the Foundation let him do anything he wished. He complained, 'I am rusty, rusty,' but did respond with a new work for soprano, mixed choir and orchestra, *Gloria*. Poulenc originally wanted seven movements in his *Gloria*, but settled for six, with a final Amen as the seventh movement, to attain the 'golden number'.

Like the *Stabat Mater, Gloria* was written for soprano solo, chorus and orchestra, yet the purposes of the two compositions were different: Stabat was a stern piece, based on the text of a poem and divided into twelve sections. *Gloria* was simpler both in structure and in its emotional message of joy. Instead of the larger architectural frame of a Baroque *Gloria* such as that of Vivaldi, which contains twelve movements, Poulenc said he had in mind the continuously interrelated structure of his cycle *La Fraîcheur et le Feu* when he chose the six movements for his *Gloria* – Gloria, Laudamus te, Domine

Deus, Domini Fili Unigenite, Domine Deus, Agnus Dei and Qui sedes ad dexteram Patris.

The merry Laudamus te was inspired, according to Poulenc, by a football match he once saw played by 'grave Benedictines' and again he invoked a favourite image, Benozzo Gozzoli's impish angels sticking out their tongues. The sinuous soprano solo, Domine Deus, was a bit of orientalia, in the tradition of Saint-Saëns. In this work, the vigour of the music is of utmost importance, even though this sometimes means it is disconnected from the words: Domine Deus, Agnus Dei has the verve of a rustic clog dance, but bears little relation to the text about Jesus.

Poulenc said that he had written enough tragedies that made people weep and he hoped to regain the energy expressed in *Les Biches* and *Les Mamelles*. As a tribute to his musical past, he had used as part of the fanfare opening of *Gloria* a melody he had written in 1928 for a minor piano work, *Hymne*; yet none of his early works is as consciously escapist as *Gloria* is at times.

One can see why *Gloria* became instantly popular in Eisenhower's America: its sunny air was like the aftermath of a perfect tranquillizer. The sedative quality to this pretty music was a sign that the idea of oblivion was starting to appeal to the composer. *Gloria*'s popularity was sometimes based on a misreading of Poulenc's life and work – the British conductor and composer of church music, John Rutter, has commented in his sleeve notes of his recording of *Gloria* that 'the essentially affirmative, optimistic nature of Poulenc's personality and faith is everywhere apparent.' But as Poulenc's life drew to a close he did not recognize these aspects in his character. He knew that he had written his masterpiece in the *Dialogues* and was starting to feel hints of what an old age in ill health and emotional insecurity would be like.

Opposite, Poulenc's *Gloria*, here shown in a posthumous British ballet version in reptilian costume, was rhythmically confident, but also reeked of an artificial serenity suggestive of the oblivion of tranquillized sleep, very familiar to Poulenc in his last years.

Poulenc wrote the soprano solos in *Gloria* with the voice of Leontyne Price in mind. Poulenc had been enchanted by a recording of some of his songs that she had made in 1959, coached by Doda Conrad's accompanist, David Garvey, and wanted her to sing the solos in *Gloria*: the arching flexible melodies were intended to be sung with the rich, sensuous Price tone, which possessed both the weight for singing Verdi and Puccini and the refinement for Richard Strauss.

As Poulenc left two full-length ballets, one might wonder why some modern choreographers set dancers moving to works not intended to be choreographed, such as *Gloria*, only to achieve results that might be described as forced and artificial.

Price accepted, but scheduling conflicts made it impossible for her to perform the piece, and when *Gloria* was given its première in January 1961 in Boston, the American soprano Adele Addison sang the solos, much to Poulenc's approval.

The performance was conducted by Charles Munch, the leader of the Boston Symphony Orchestra, and in rehearsals Poulenc was full of patronizing comments about 'the dear, the adorable, the exquisite Charlie who understood nothing' about *Gloria*. Poulenc felt that Munch only understood Honegger and Roussel: 'How "Strasbourg" he is, the dear treasure!' The performance overall was a success, but Poulenc seemed most fascinated at Marlene Dietrich's arrival in the 'sinister city' of Boston for the première, to pose for photographs kissing him. Today, *Gloria* is the second most-performed piece of French music in the world, surpassed only by Ravel's *Boléro*, according to the French composer's union SACEM.

Poulenc was often involved in deep friendships with both partners of a married couple. The American soprano Rose Dercourt-Plaut had a crush on Poulenc, who was in turn smitten by Rose's husband, Fred Plaut, who took this photograph.

Once *Gloria* was completed, indecision about musical projects permitted him to write a book he had long planned, in homage to Chabrier, for a series published by Les Éditions du Seuil in Paris. Poulenc's essay turned out to be too short for the collection, and the composer did not want to spend time to make it longer; the book was finally produced by a small publisher in Switzerland.

Casting about for projects, Poulenc tried his hand at a choral work about a saint whom he admired since his youth, *Laudes de Saint Antoine de Padoue* (1959). In the small-scale work in four movements for men's voices *a cappella*, a Gregorian influence clashed with a more sinuous charm, in the University singing group style. It was as if Poulenc were returning to the well of inspiration of his 1922 *Chanson à boire*, only to find it dry: even St Anthony of Padua could not help his disarray.

At the end of 1959, Leonard Bernstein comissioned Poulenc to write an orchestral work for the opening of the new Philharmonic Hall at Lincoln Center in New York. Refreshed by his break after writing the Chabrier book, Poulenc transcended his problems to create his last major work, *Sept Répons des ténèbres* for boy soprano, mixed choir (boys and men) and orchestra.

For his Latin texts, Poulenc chose parts of evening services for holy week, plus readings from the Lamentations of Jeremiah, Saint Augustine, and the Epistles of Saint Paul. Even more than *La Voix humaine*, *Sept Répons* proved that for Poulenc, there was musical life after *Dialogues des Carmélites.*

Sept Répons showed a will to experiment in sound, with solo boy soprano and boy choir, which he had never written for in religious music. Instead of repeating once again the formula of woman soprano, chorus and orchestra, Poulenc's choice of a boy soprano may have been a recollection of Falla's use of a rough-voiced peasant lad in his *El retablo* decades before. Poulenc said he did not want a boy soprano who sounded upper class, from the ritzy *Plaine Monceau* quarter of Paris, 'appropriate for Fauré's music for dead rich people. I want the son of a *La Villette* butcher or plumber (with a deeper tessitura).'

Ever the professional, Poulenc tried to cover every eventuality: if a good boy soprano was unavailable, he suggested that a reedy tenor, of the Hugues Cuénod style, could be substituted. Along with Falla's work, Poulenc's acknowledged model was the choral music of the Spanish composer Victoria. Perhaps because of this sustained Spanish influence, *Sept Répons* had a dramatic atmosphere that was lacking in *Gloria.*

There was plenty of angry writing for brass, and urgent music for the boy soloist, not the ethereal, disembodied style of the earlier work. Poulenc claimed that he wanted to destroy music he had written which was too pretty and return to 'the austerity and violence I wanted at the beginning'. The beginnings Poulenc referred to were his early works with raw anguish, like *Le Bal masqué.* Like the First Prioress in *Dialogues des Carmélites,* Poulenc found a religious atmosphere no consolation, faced by the proximity of death.

Opposite, ever sedentary, Poulenc despised taking country walks, which he claimed depressed him: he stayed at Noizay in order to work, drink the local wine and entertain his friends and lovers.

The first movement of *Sept Répons* harkens back to the *Litanies à la Vierge noire.* Speaking of the betrayal of Jesus by Judas, the music conveys real rage. However, the sixth movement, Sepulto Domino, is joyous music, speaking of the burial of Jesus by Nicodemus as a tender act of love. At the end of the movement, the voices fade away: for the just man, death is a descent to the tomb with Jesus. There are parallels with the message of Bach's aria 'Mache dich, mein' herze rein' ('Make thee clean, my heart') from the Saint Matthew Passion. Henri Hell aptly called *Sept Répons* 'a kind of *Passion* in miniature'.

Poulenc saw his work as visual as well as aural, although only he knew precisely what certain references to painters meant: He said that *Sept Répons* was more Mantegna than Zurbarán, although he would have liked to achieve a Holbein effect. He particularly admired Zurbarán's 'ascetic purity which nevertheless is not afraid to dress up some women saints as important ladies'. Such comparisons of painting and music were more useful to the composer for creating an emotional atmosphere, than they are to the listener who may think of other painters, or none at all, in hearing the *Sept Répons.* Whatever the exact sense of these general parallels which he often insisted upon, Poulenc correctly saw the *Sept Répons* as 'very interior, not at all decorative like the *Gloria*'.

Clearly the composer was meditating on final things; the work was given its première after Poulenc's death, in April 1963 by the New York

Philharmonic conducted by Thomas Schippers. Yet unlike other posthumous compositions, the *Sept Répons* are not the last gasp of an exhausted talent, but rather a rallying of forces.

After *Sept Répons*, Poulenc wavered once again with a song cycle for Denise Duval to sing to her son. *La Courte Paille* (1960) was set to sentimental poems by a Belgian children's writer, Maurice Carême (1899-1977). Poulenc found this writer comparable to Francis Jammes and Max Jacob, whereas he was in fact inferior to these two writers, with embarrassing lines such as 'under the fingers of angel musicians, Mozart drips deliciously in droplets of blue joy.'

La Courte Paille contained seven songs: 'Le Sommeil,' 'Quelle Aventure!', 'La Reine de cœur', 'Ba, be, bi, bo, bu', 'Les Anges musiciens', 'Le Carafon', and 'Lune d'avril'. They are neurotic cradle songs, with the singer as mother bringing sleep to the little ones, while children's death is evoked, and an ice maiden as dangerous as Schubert's *Erlkönig*. Poulenc's music alternately communicates lax abandonment or edgy nervousness; the emotional climate of the music may have been linked to whether the tranquillizers he was taking worked or not on a given day.

As he did with Eluard, Poulenc asked Carême to suggest possible titles for the cycle, and the Belgian poet's ideas included 'Brigolette', 'Piccolo Piccola', 'Furidondaine Furidondon', 'Lorelirelé', 'Cahin-caha', 'Églantine enfantine' and many others. Coming from the composer of the delicious *Babar*, and the Four Songs for Children, *La Courte Paille* was a saccharine disappointment. Duval disliked the work and refused to sing it, saying lamely that they were not right for her voice, hardly believable, given Poulenc's knowledge of her singing: not only did he write operas for her, but he also gave detailed advice before she sang major roles like Mélisande.

Fortunately, *La Courte Paille* was not Poulenc's last vocal composition for Duval. *La Dame de Monte Carlo*, a monologue for soprano and piano (or orchestra) lasts under seven minutes in performance. It is comic-pathetic in theme: an ageing woman of the world who has lost her looks, her luck bemoans her past glory, before commiting suicide by leaping in the Mediterranean. The stage monologue was written by Jean Cocteau in the 1930s in rigid rhyming form, almost as archaic as Louis Aragon's 'C'. To avoid monotony, the composer deliberately tried to vary the musical mood with each couplet: 'Melancholy, pride, lyricism, violence, and sarcasm and plunk into the ocean!'

The orchestration is subtle and discreet, with doubled wind, strings, and percussion, similar to the orchestration of *La Voix humaine*; tam-tam, castanets, and vibraphone are introduced intermittently to bolster the vocal line. Despite the potentially absurd subject matter, Poulenc's setting was restrained and delicate: at times its seriousness recalls *La Voix humaine*, when La Dame sings, 'et maintenant, c'est moi qui vous parle.' Like Elle in *La Voix humaine*, La Dame is also a nameless woman with a common, unhappy fate. Both attempt suicide as solutions to their abandonment. Some of Poulenc's friends like Bernac felt *La Dame* to be trivial, perhaps because of its self-pity about a common gay theme – Poulenc could easily identify with an ugly old thing who needed to pay for company, 'to hire a rigolo', (a playful way of referring to a gigolo as a 'funny fellow' in rhyming slang). In some of Poulenc's late photographs, he is almost startlingly homely, like French screen actors who based careers on their mugs, such as Fernandel or Michel Simon. He would tell friends, 'essentially, I'm just an old *grue*.' More literally than in *Dialogues* or *La Voix humaine*, Poulenc wrote about himself in the character of La Dame. La Dame is the sort of merciless late self-portrait Rembrandt might have made, had he been gay, a composer, and French.

Poulenc said that *La Dame de Monte Carlo* should be sung like Tosca's aria *Vissi d'arte*, the ultimate aria of victimization, in which the singer says she has lived for art and love, and asks why terrible things are happening to her: *La Dame de Monte Carlo* was not written to emotional scale for Denise Duval: she was too young and pretty at the time to fit the character, although she performed it superlatively in December 1961, with an orchestra conducted by Georges Prêtre. The characterful cantata needs a stagewise performer like Felicity Lott, who recorded the piano version with Graham Johnson.

Poulenc's last stage collaboration was with Jean Cocteau, for his play *Renaud et Armide*, staged at the Festival of Baalbek in August 1962. Disenchanted with the project, Poulenc declared he would

This photograph depicts what seems like an old and happy marriage, but Poulenc discovered his friend Jean Cocteau's work only late in life, setting Cocteau's play *La Voix humaine* and the stage monologue *La Dame de Monte Carlo* among his last compositions.

write 'a few farts' for the play which 'bored' him. Poulenc's last two substantial works were solo sonatas for wind instruments. Through a strange sort of symmetry that appeals to reference book writers, Debussy (1862-1918) and Saint-Saëns (1835-1921) also ended their careers with chamber music sonatas. However, Debussy's included string works, and would have reached six works had not death intervened. Debussy had a nationalistic French program to convey in his work that was far from the political indifference of Poulenc and Saint-Saëns.

For parallels to Poulenc's last sonatas, Saint-Saëns was closer; at the age of eighty-six, Saint-Saëns penned sonatas for oboe, clarinet, and bassoon. The French musicologist Jean-Alexandre Ménétrier states that the finale of Saint-Saëns's oboe sonata prefigures Poulenc, in its 'witty charm'. The Saint-Saëns work was written just when Poulenc started his career after World War I. Saint-Saëns's clarinet sonata has more sober, valedictory moments, in key with the elegiac nature of Poulenc's last works.

Poulenc's Sonata for clarinet and piano is like his Flute Sonata in combining virtuoso writing with lyric flow: it has a touch of German Romanticism via Weber that at times give it a spooky air. In three movements, Allegro tristamente, Romanza and Allegro con fuoco, the work has a certain classical reserve. The central romanza is a stately sarabande, while the rapid finale is dynamic, yet anxious. In its fast–slow–fast structure, the Clarinet Sonata resembled the Flute Sonata. In both sonatas, emotional moods of individual movements were similar: after movements of melancholy lyricism, the second movements were bel canto 'Cantilène' while the Finales were high-stepping popular melodies. The Clarinet Sonata was given its première on 10 April 1963 at Carnegie Hall by Benny Goodman, accompanied by Leonard Bernstein.

A far more interiorized work, the Sonata for oboe and piano (1962) has three movements, 'Elégie', 'Scherzo', and 'Déploration'. The Oboe Sonata is a work of suggestions rather than statements, which we overhear as much as hear. The confidences of an oboe are given to us as if at the end of a long day, when someone sits opposite you and speaks frankly of what is in his heart. The unusual emotional communicativeness of the 'Déploration' movement is a *memento*

Opposite, Camille Saint-Saëns, whose late sonatas for wind instruments prefigure the 'witty charm' of those by Poulenc

mori, intimating that player and listener alike must someday die. The sonata's unusual structure of slow–fast–slow movements leaves a sombre conclusion: in this sense, the Oboe Sonata is closer to the Sonata for two pianos or the *Elégie* for horn and piano, than to the other wind sonatas, for clarinet and flute, which were written around the same time. The Oboe Sonata was given its première by Pierre Pierlot accompanied by Jacques Février in June 1963, at the Strasbourg Music Festival.

The Oboe and Clarinet Sonatas, in their absence of development of themes, rejected classical models: they were dedicated to the memories of the recently dead Arthur Honegger and Sergey Prokofiev, respectively. Poulenc felt a link between his wind sonatas and the dead (as in the homage to Dennis Brain in the *Elégie* for horn). This morbid aspect may have stemmed from Raymonde Linossier's great fondness for wind instruments, and her urging Francis to compose in this format.

After all these heavy forbodings, death surprised Poulenc, but perhaps not really. Poulenc, who had had such a delightful life, was granted an ideal death: he dropped dead of a heart attack in his Paris apartment on the rue des Medicis, on 30 January 1963. That very day, he was planning to lunch with Denise Duval and record some more radio broadcasts with his old friend Stéphane Audel. He cancelled lunch because he had a bad cold, and at 1 p.m. his sudden heart attack occurred. He had vacated his Paris apartment for all of November 1962 so that it could be painted. Either he did not expect to die, or having premonitions, he gallantly had his apartment redone in order to leave it in spiffy shape to his heirs. The heavy doses of mood-altering drugs he had gobbled for years – French psychiatrists are notorious for overmedicating their patients –may have weakened his heart. Yet heredity, an important factor in longevity, may also have determined that Poulenc died at almost the same age as his father had.

Four days before his death, he accompanied Duval in a recital at Maastricht. After the concert, he chivalrously sent flowers to her hotel room with a note that said, 'My Denise, I owe you my last (latest) joy. Your poor Fr.' No unfinished works were discovered after his death, further evidence that he organized things before the end. The funeral, on 2 February 1963 was at Saint-Sulpice, followed by burial at the Père

Lachaise cemetery. No music of Poulenc's was performed for the occasion, at the request of the composer. Instead, Marcel Dupré performed Bach at the great organ of Saint-Sulpice. François Mauriac, a long-time friend, wrote about Poulenc's funeral, quoting a maxim, 'Tell me how you are buried and I'll tell you who you are,' which was untrue about Mozart, Schubert, and any number of composers who were not as rich as Poulenc. Nevertheless the reassuringly wealthy atmosphere of a large-scale ceremony at Saint-Sulpice was representative of Poulenc's well-upholstered life. Perhaps a clearer sign of the deep attachment Poulenc inspired in his circle was the suicide of his housekeeper, Suzanne Rocheron, shortly after the composer's death; she and her husband had worked for him since 1928, and she could not overcome the pain of his loss, nor contemplate leaving the house at Noizay.

Years later, Pierre Bernac confessed that the first thing Poulenc's friends did on meeting one another was to talk about Poulenc, as if he were still among them. Few, even among his ardent admirers, would have expected the world-wide popularity he now enjoys. New recordings constantly appear, and major record companies like EMI and Sony still hold on to dozens of unreprinted recordings of performances by Poulenc himself and Bernac, which may someday be a further reason to admire this multi-gifted musician.

What is Poulenc's status as a composer at the end of his century? It rather depends on whom you ask. There is no stern super-ego saying that you *must* like a certain work by Poulenc, otherwise you are impossibly primitive, backward, and un-chic. Poulenc's work stands on its own charms, unlike a lot of the avant-garde, which people listen to because they are ashamed to get up and leave the concert hall. From early in his career, Poulenc's music was accepted as amusing, but eclectic, heavily inspired by Stravinsky and others. The American song composer Ned Rorem wrote in *Opera News*: 'Though Poulenc never penned an original note, every note became pure Poulenc through some witty alchemy.'

Overpraise was also a danger. A New Yorker critic reviewed a Poulenc memorial concert in April 1963, calling him 'a true genius and certainly one of the greatest of all twentieth-century composers. The conservatism of his style was simply a matter of preference.' More

Following page, until the end of his life, Poulenc was always happy to get into contact with young admirers, if not always for entirely altruistic reasons, such as here, where he is pictured at a meeting of French record collectors in 1962.

L'HISTOIRE
BABAR
BAR

FRANCIS POULENC
FRANCIS POULENC

Babar and Céleste rise gracefully into the distance: the sheer fun of Poulenc's *Babar* permeates many of his works and is his enduring legacy.

often, the praise handed out to Poulenc is qualified, such as calling him one of the members of Les Six whose music is most likely to survive.

There was no 'school of Poulenc' among composers of following generations. During his lifeitme and afterwards, his music was inimitable, because so firmly based on his particular personality. No one in France has followed Poulenc's example in writing lyric melodies. Younger composers whom he admired and encouraged, such as Henri Dutilleux and Pierre Boulez, have followed their own paths without any musical debt to Poulenc. In America, Ned Rorem and Leonard Bernstein benefited from Poulenc's proof that art songs could be written in our time in a tonal, accessible idiom. More recent tonal composers in America, like David Del Tredici and John Corigliano, have also learned from this example although Rorem and the latter two composers' output was vastly inferior to Poulenc's in quality. The idea of a tonal opera like *Dialogues des Carmélites*, with no concessions to the avant-garde, may have also given courage to traditionalist modern opera composers like Thea Musgrave. No-one has quite matched Poulenc's range – from songs to ballets to operas; no-one has written music as scandalously life-enjoying as *Les Biches*. The only contemporary who reached the samc level of wild enjoyment and juicy emotion was Milhaud, in his ballets *Le Boeuf sur le toit* and *La Création du monde*.

Since then, French music has had other priorities. France's appetite for Cartesian reflection and intellectual 'research' has dominated in the latter half of the twentieth century, embodied in the sparse, often ungratifying works of Boulez. It is hard not to sense a drying-up of musical inspiration, if not in intelligence, among French composers in the post-Poulenc era. After him, *le dessèchement*!

Poulenc repeatedly insisted that his music must be loved, not analyzed. He ended his endearing book about the composer Chabrier with the words, 'Dear Chabrier, how we love you!' Clearly he would have liked the same message addressed to himself by admirers. Were Poulenc alive today he would admire the labours of love by Myriam Chimènes and Sidney Buckland in collecting, annotating, and translating his letters, and the painstaking publication of his book, *Journal de mes mélodies*, by the critic Renaud Machart. Such conductors as Robert Shaw, Manuel Rosenthal, and Georges Prêtre have continued performing his music into old age; and in 1995 Paris enjoyed Poulenc's *Babar* splendidly narrated by two friends of the composer, both of whom were born in 1902: the Swiss tenor Hugues Cuénod, and Madeleine Milhaud, the widow of Poulenc's friend Darius. The composer's niece Rosine Seringe chairs a Paris group, Les amis de Francis Poulenc; an ardent group of Poulenc fans from Kansas City, MO, run by Catharine Strom, Friends of Francis Poulenc USA, organizes concerts and sells sweatshirts, coffee mugs and refrigerator magnets with the composer's image on them.

Perhaps Francis Poulenc would now be able to conclude that he *is* loved, after all.

Classified List of Works

Poulenc produced an enormous amount of music during his career, some of which added little of significance to his œuvre. The 'best of Poulenc', as the composer himself liked to say, was what he would be remembered by. Many of Poulenc's piano works were written for commercial purposes and were despised by the composer. Although listed here, they have not been commented upon in the present book. Myriam Chimènes's edition of Poulenc's *Correspondance* is a highly valuable source of information about Poulenc's work. A catalogue of Poulenc's works by the American musicologist Carl B. Schmidt has recently been published by Oxford University Press, and will no doubt be of primary importance to Poulenc studies in the future. The following list denotes first public performances by 'fp', and gives details where known.

Stage Works

'Discours du général' and 'La Baigneuse de Trouville' in *Les Mariés de la Tour Eiffel*, libretto by Jean Cocteau (1921). fp Paris, 18 June 1921

Le Gendarme incompris, 'comédie-bouffe' in one act, text by Jean Cocteau and Raymond Radiguet (1921). fp Paris, May 1921

Les Biches, ballet in one act (1923). fp Monte Carlo, 6 January 1924

'Pastourelle' in *L'Éventail de Jeanne* (1927). fp Paris, 4 March 1929

Aubade, 'concerto choréographique' for piano and eighteen instruments (1929). fp Paris, 1 December 1929 (concert version); Paris, 21 January 1930 (stage version)

Les Animaux modèles, ballet in one act after La Fontaine (1940–1). fp Paris, 8 August 1942

Les Mamelles de Tirésias, 'opéra bouffe' in a prologue and two acts, libretto by Guillaume Apollinaire (1944). fp Paris, 3 June 1947

Dialogues des Carmélites, opera in three acts, libretto by Georges Bernanos (1953–6). fp Milan, 26 January 1957 (in Italian); Paris, 21 June 1957 (in French)

La Voix humaine, 'tragédie lyrique' in one act, libretto by Jean Cocteau (1958). fp Paris, 6 February 1959

Orchestral

Concert champêtre, for harpsichord and orchestra (1927–8). fp Paris, 3 May 1929

Concerto for Two Pianos (1932). fp Venice, 5 September 1932

Suite française d'après Claude Gervaise, for six wind instruments, harpsichord and percussion (1935). fp Paris, 11 December 1935

Deux Marches et un intermède, for chamber orchestra (1937). fp Paris, 3 April 1938

Concerto for Organ, Strings and Timpani (1938). fp Paris, 21 June 1939

Deux Préludes posthumes et une gnossienne, orchestration of piano pieces by Erik Satie (1939)

Suite from *Les Biches* (1939–40)

Suite from *Les Animaux modèles* (1942)

Sinfonietta (1947–8). fp London, 24 October 1948

Piano Concerto (1949). fp Boston, 6 January 1950

'Matelote provençale', variation on a theme by Campra from the eighteenth-century opera *Camille* (1952). fp Aix-en-Provence, 31 July 1952

'Bucolique', for orchestra, from *Variations sur le nom de Marguerite Long* (1956). fp Paris, 4 June 1956

Renaud et Armide, stage music for play by Jean Cocteau (1962). fp Baalbek, August 1962

Choral

Chanson à boire, for male chorus *a cappella*, eighteenth-century anonymous poem (1922)

Sept Chansons, texts by Guillaume Apollinaire, Paul Eluard and Jean Legrand (1936). fp Paris, 21 May 1937

Litanies à la Vierge noire, for chorus and organ (1936). fp London, 17 November 1936

Petites Voix, for children's chorus *a cappella* (1936)

Mass in G, for mixed chorus *a cappella* (1937). fp Paris, 3 April 1938

Sécheresses, cantata for chorus and orchestra, texts by Edward James (1937). fp Paris, 2 May 1938

Quatre Motets pour un temps de Pénitence, for mixed chorus *a cappella* (1938–9). fp Paris, February 1939

Exultante Deo, for mixed chorus *a cappella* (1941)

Salve Regina, for mixed chorus *a cappella* (1941)

Figure humaine, cantata for double chorus, text by Paul Eluard (1943; revised 1959). fp London, 25 March 1945

Un Soir de neige, chamber cantata, text by Paul Eluard (1944). fp Paris, 21 April 1945

Chansons françaises, mixed chorus (1945–6)

Quatre Petits Prières de Saint François d'Assise, for male voice choir (1948). fp 1949

Stabat Mater, for soprano solo, chorus and orchestra (1950). fp Strasbourg, 13 June 1951

Quatre Motets pour un temps de Noël, for mixed chorus *a cappella* (1951–2)

Ave verum corpus, for women's choir (1952). fp Pittsburgh, Pennsylvania, 25 November 1952

Laudes de Saint Antoine de Padoue, for male voice choir *a cappella* (1957–9)

Gloria, for soprano solo, chorus and orchestra (1959). fp Boston, 20 January 1961

Sept Répons des ténèbres, for boy soprano and male chorus with orchestra (1961–2). fp New York, 11 April 1963

Vocal with Piano

(except where stated otherwise)

Rapsodie nègre, for baritone, piano, string quartet, flute and clarinet, nonsense text by Francis Poulenc in pseudo-African dialect (1917; revised 1933). fp Paris, 11 December 1917

Toréador, text by Jean Cocteau (1918; revised 1932)

Le Bestiaire, text by Guillaume Apollinaire (1919). fp Paris, 1919

Cocardes, for voice, cornet, trombone, bass drum, triangle and violin, text by Jean Cocteau (1919; revised 1939). fp Paris, 21 February 1920

Quatre Poèmes de Max Jacob, for voice, flute, oboe, clarinet, bassoon and trumpet (1921). fp Paris, 7 January 1922

Cinq Poèmes de Ronsard, text by Pierre de Ronsard (1924–5). fp Paris, 10 March 1925

Chansons gaillardes, anonymous seventeenth-century texts (1925–6). fp Paris, 2 May 1926

Vocalise (1927). fp 7 May 1927

Airs chantés, text by Jean Moréas (1927–8). fp Paris, 10 June 1928

'Epitaphe', text by François de Malherbe (1930)

Trois Poèmes de Louise Lalanne, text by Marie Laurencin and Guillaume Apollinaire (1931). fp Paris, 1 June 1931

Quatre Poèmes de Guillaume Apollinaire (1931). fp Paris, 1 June 1931

Cinq Poèmes de Max Jacob (1931). fp Paris, 24 May 1932

Le Bal masqué, cantata for baritone or mezzo-soprano and chamber ensemble (1932). fp Hyères, 20 April 1932

Huit Chansons polonaises (1934)

Quatre Chansons pour enfants (1934)

Cinq Poèmes de Paul Eluard (1935). fp Paris, 3 April 1935

'À Sa Guitare', text by Pierre de Ronsard (1935)

Tel Jour, telle nuit, text by Paul Eluard (1936–7). fp Paris, 3 February 1937

Trois Poèmes de Louise de Vilmorin (1937). fp Paris, 28 November 1938

'Le Portrait', text by Colette (1938). fp Paris, 16 February 1939

Deux Poèmes de Guillaume Apollinaire (1938). fp Paris, 16 February 1939

'Priez pour paix', text by Charles d'Orléans (1938)

'La Grenouillière', text by Guillaume Apollinaire (1938)

Miroirs brûlants, text by Paul Eluard (1938–9). fp Paris, 16 February 1939

'Ce doux petit visage', text by Paul Eluard (1939). fp Paris, 9 December 1940

Fiançailles pour rire, text by Louise de Vilmorin (1939). fp Paris, 21 May 1942

Bleuet, text by Guillaume Apollinaire (1939)

Les Chemins de l'amour, 'valse chantée' from *Léocadia*, text by Jean Anouilh (1940). fp Paris, 3 November 1940

Banalités, text by Guillaume Apollinaire (1940). fp Paris, 14 December 1940

Colloque, for soprano and baritone, text by Paul Valéry (1940). fp Paris, 4 February 1941

Chansons villageoises, for voice and orchestra, text by Maurice Fombeure (1942). fp Paris, 28 June 1943

Métamorphoses, text by Louise de Vilmorin (1943). fp Paris, 8 December 1943

Deux Poèmes de Louis Aragon (1943). fp Paris, 8 December 1943

'Montparnasse' and 'Hyde Park', texts by Guillaume Apollinaire (1941–5). fp Paris, 27 April 1945

'Le Pont' and 'Un Poème', texts by Guillaume Apollinaire (1946). fp Paris, 6 November 1946

'Paul et Virginie', text by Raymond Radiguet (1946)

'Le Disparu', text by Robert Desnos (1946–7)

'Main dominée par le cœur', text by Paul Eluard (1946–7)

Trois Chansons, text by Federico García Lorca (1947). fp Paris, 12 November 1947

'... Mais Mourir', text by Paul Eluard (1947)

Calligrammes, text by Guillaume Apollinaire (1948). fp New York, 20 November 1948

'Hymne', text by Jean Racine (1948–9). fp New York, 28 December 1948

Mazurka, text by Louise de Vilmorin (1949). fp New York, 6 November 1949

La Fraîcheur et le Feu, text by Paul Eluard (1950). fp Birmingham, 1 November 1950

Parisiana, text by Max Jacob (1954). fp Amsterdam, 12 October 1954

'Rosemonde', text by Guillaume Apollinaire (1954). fp Amsterdam, 12 October 1954

Le Travail du peintre, text by Paul Eluard (1956). fp Paris, 1 April 1957

Deux Mélodies (1956). fp 5 September 1957

'Dernier Poème', text by Robert Desnos (1956)

'Une Chanson de porcelaine', text by Paul Eluard (1958)

'Fancy', text by William Shakespeare (1959)

La Courte Paille, text by Maurice Carême (1960). fp L'Abbaye de Royaumont, 1961

La Dame de Monte Carlo, monologue for soprano and orchestra, libretto by Jean Cocteau (1961). fp Monte Carlo, November 1961

Narrator and piano

L'Histoire de Babar, le petit éléphant, text by Jean de Brunhoff (1940–45). fp Paris, 14 June 1946 (radio); London, 8 February 1949 (public)

Chamber

Sonata for two clarinets (1918; revised 1945). fp Paris, 5 April 1919

Sonata for clarinet and bassoon (1922; revised 1945). fp Paris, 4 January 1923

Sonata for horn, trumpet and trombone (1922; revised 1945). fp Paris, 4 January 1923

Trio for oboe, bassoon and piano (1926). fp Paris, 2 May 1926

Sextet for piano and winds (1932–9). fp Paris, 19 June 1932

Léocadia, for voice, clarinet, bassoon, violin, double bass and piano, music to play by Jean Anouilh (1940). fp Paris, 3 November 1940

Instrumental

'Villanelle' from *Pipeaux*, for one pipe and piano (1934)

Sonata for violin and piano (1942–3; corrected edition 1949). fp Paris, 21 June 1943

Sonata for cello and piano (1948; corrected edition 1953). fp Paris, 18 May 1949

Sonata for flute and piano (1956–7). fp Strasbourg, 18 June 1957

Elégie for horn and piano (1957). fp London, 17 February 1958 (radio)

Sarabande for guitar (1960)

Sonata for clarinet and piano (1962). fp New York, 10 April 1963

Sonata for oboe and piano (1962). fp Strasbourg, 8 June 1963

Piano

Sonata for piano duet (1918; revised 1939). fp Paris, 21 February 1920

Trois Mouvements perpétuels (1918; revised 1939 and 1962). fp Paris, 9 February 1919

'Valse' from *Album des Six* (1914–19). fp Paris, 1919

Suite for piano (1920; revised 1926). fp Paris, 10 April 1920

Six Impromptus (1920–1; revised 1939). fp Paris, 22 February 1922

Promenades (1921; revised 1952). fp Paris, 7 May 1923

Napoli (1922–5). fp Paris, 2 May 1926

Deux Novellettes (1927–8; revised 1939). fp Paris, 10 June 1928

Trois Pièces (1918–28; revised 1953). fp Paris, 10 June 1928

'Pièce brève sur le nom d'Albert Roussel' from *Hommage à Albert Roussel* (1929). fp Paris, 18 April 1929

Nocturnes (1929–38)

'Valse-improvisation sur le nom de Bach' from *Hommage à J. S. Bach* (1932)

Improvisations (1932–34). fp Paris, 4 February 1933

Villageoises (1933)

Feuillets d'album (1933)

Presto (1934)

Deux Intermezzi (1934)

Humoresque (1934)

Badinage (1934)

Suite française d'après Claude Gervaise; keyboard arrangement of *Suite française* for small orchestra (1935).

Les Soirées de Nazelles (1930–36). fp London, 1 February 1936

'Bourrée au Pavillon d'Auvergne' from *À l'Exposition* (1937). fp Paris, 24 June 1937

Mélancolie (1940). fp Paris, 23 May 1941

Intermezzo (1943)

L'Embarquement pour Cythère, valse-musette (1951)

Thème varié (1951). fp Paris, 15 December 1952

Sonata for two pianos (1952–3). fp London, 2 November 1953

Élegie for two pianos (1959)

Novelette, on a theme by Manuel de Falla (1959)

Further Reading

The recent edition of Poulenc's *Correspondance*, edited by Myriam Chimènes, adds a work to French literature. Her research – and that of others – has corrected some of Poulenc's statements in his book of conversations, particularly concerning World War II. France's Institut National de l'Audiovisuel has reprinted on two CDs an edited version of the original radio conversations which were partly transcribed for Poulenc's *Entretiens avec Claude Rostand*. This reprint, as with other valuable recent items in the Poulenc bibliography, was the brainchild of French music critic Renaud Machart. Stéphane Audel's book of chats is the most appealing of the original sources, while Henri Hell's biography remains the most trustworthy as regards strictly musical matters. Of recent books in English, the most informative is Sidney Buckland's admirable translation of the letters. Wilfred Mellers's study is touching in its sincere enthusiasm, particularly for the piano works. The following list selects the most accurate and amusing publications by Poulenc as well as the most readily available works on the composer in both French and English.

Writings by Poulenc

record reviews in *Arts phoniques*, No. 5, June 1928

'Oeuvres récentes de Darius Milhaud' in *Contrepoints*, No. 1, January 1946

'La musique de piano de Prokofiev' in *Musique russe* (Paris, Presses Universitaires de France, 1953)

Correspondance 1915–1963, ed. Hélène de Wendel (Paris, Seuil, 1967)

Echo and Source: Selected Correspondence 1915–1963, trans. and ed. S. Buckland (London, Gollancz, 1991)

Correspondance 1910–1963, ed. M. Chimènes (Paris, Fayard, 1994). This collection supersedes the volumes cited above; for English readers, an augmented version of Sidney Buckland's collection is clearly called for.

Emmanuel Chabrier (Paris & Geneva, La Palatine, 1961)

Francis Poulenc: Entretiens avec Claude Rostand (Paris, Julliard, 1954)

Diary of my Songs (*Journal de mes mélodies*), trans. W. Radford, intro. G. Johnson (London, Gollancz, 1989)

Journal de mes mélodies, ed. R. Machart (Paris, Cicero, 1993). Poulenc's notes not only about his songs, but about the rest of his music, his friends and life in general. Machart discovered that about a third of Poulenc's *Journal* was not included in the 1964 edition. This new edition incorporates an important amount of unknown material and merits translation into English.

Moi et mes amis, ed. S. Audel (Paris & Geneva, La Palatine, 1963)

My Friends and Myself (*Moi et mes amis*), ed. S. Audel, trans. J. Harding (London, Dennis Dobson, 1978)

Writings about Poulenc

Auric, G. *Quand j'étais là* (Paris, Grasset, 1979)

Bernac, P. *Francis Poulenc, the Man and his Songs*, trans. W. Radford (London, Gollancz & New York, Norton, 1977)

Bernac, P. *Francis Poulenc et ses mélodies* (Paris, Buchet-Chastel, 1978)

Bloch, F. *Phonographies II, Francis Poulenc, 1928–1982* (Paris, Bibliothèque Nationale, Départment de Phonothèque Nationale et de l'Audiovisuel, 1984)

Brooks, J. 'Nadia Boulanger and the Salon of the Princesse de Polignac' in *Journal of the American Musicological Society*, Vol. XLVI, No. 3, 1993

Cocteau, J. *Cahier Jean Cocteau no. 7, avec les musiciens* (Paris, Gallimard, 1978)

— 'Les Biches ... notes de Monte Carlo' in *La Nouvelle Revue française*, No. 126, 1924

— *Le Passé défini, tomes I–III, 1951–54* (Paris, Gallimard, 1983–9)

Collaer, P. *Darius Milhaud* (Geneva and Paris, Slatkine, 1989)

Craft, R. (ed.) *Igor Stravinsky, Selected Correspondence, Volume III* (London, Faber and Faber, 1985)

Crespin, R., D. Duval et al. 'Poulenc. Dialogues des Carmélites, La Voix humaine' in *Avant scène d'Opéra*, No. 52, May 1983

Daniels, K. W. *Francis Poulenc, His Artistic Development and Musical Style* (UMI Research Press, 1982)

Duruflé, M. 'Le concerto pour orgue et orchestre à cordes de Francis Poulenc' in *L'Orgue*, No. 154, April–June 1975

Gallois, J. *Les Polignac: Mécènes du XXième siècle* (Monaco, Rocher, 1995)

Gold, A. and Fizdale, R. *Misia* (Paris, Gallimard, 1981)

Halbreich, H. *Arthur Honegger* (Paris, Fayard, 1978)

Hell, H. *Francis Poulenc,* trans. E. Lockspeiser (New York, Grove Press, 1959)

— *Francis Poulenc* (Paris, Fayard, 1978)

Hoffelé, J.-C. *Manuel de Falla* (Paris, Fayard, 1993)

Hoffelé, J.-C. and Kaminski, P. *Les indispensables du disque compact classique* (Paris, Fayard, 1995)

Jourdan-Morhange, H. *Mes amis musiciens* (Paris, Éditeurs Français Réunis, 1955)

Keck, G. *Francis Poulenc, a Bio-bibliography* (New York & London, Greenwood Press, 1990)

Machart, R. *Francis Poulenc* (Paris, Seuil, 'Solfèges' series, 1995)

Mellers, W. *Francis Poulenc* (Oxford, OUP, 1993)

Milhaud, D. *Ma Vie heureuse* (Paris, Belfond, 1987)

— *Entretiens avec Claude Rostand* (Paris, Belfond, 1992)

Monnier, A. *Rue de l'Odéon* (Paris, Albin Michel, 1989)

'Poulenc et ses amis': *Revue internationale de musique française* vol. 31 (Paris, Champion, 1994)

Robert F. *Louis Durey, l'aîné des Six* (Paris, Éditeurs Français Réunis, 1968)

Roy, J. *Francis Poulenc, l'homme et son œuvre* (Paris, Seghers, 1964)

— *Darius Milhaud* (Paris, Seghers, 1968)

— *Le Groupe des Six* (Paris, Seuil, 1994)

Sams, J. 'Poulenc Songs' in A. Blyth (ed.) *Song on Record 2* (Cambridge, CUP, 1988)

Sauguet, H. *La Musique, ma vie* (Paris, Librairie Séguier, 1990)

Schmidt, C. B. *Catalogue of the Compositions of Francis Poulenc* (Oxford, OUP, 1995)

Schneider, M. *L'Éternité fragile* (Vol. 3: 'Le Palais des mirages') (Paris, Grasset, 1992)

Shapiro, R. *Germaine Tailleferre* (Winston-Salem, Greenwood Press, 1993)

Vidal, P. *Francis Poulenc et les poètes* (Paris, Bibliothèque Nationale de France, cahiers d'une exposition, 1995)

Selective Discography

The best performances to date of Poulenc's operas have been conducted by Georges Prêtre and Pierre Dervaux. However, the world première performances of *Dialogues des Carmélites*, sung in Italian at La Scala, certainly merit reissue on CD; and a new version of *Les Mamelles de Tirésias* is overdue, as none has been made since the original in 1953. The piano works have been recorded by performers Poulenc adored, such as Arthur Rubinstein, Vladimir Horowitz, Marcelle Meyer and Jacques Février. (A number of Février's records for EMI await CD transfer.) Sony owns the copyright for Poulenc's own performances of his piano music, but these records are unfortunately out of print. EMI has released a poor 'complete' songs CD set, yet the company owns the rights to over one hundred songs by Poulenc and others, recorded by Poulenc and Bernac at their peak, which would be a revelation on CD. The baritone Gilbert-Moryn, who sang the première performance of *Le Bal masqué*, recorded the *Chansons gaillardes*; this would be precious evidence of early interpretation if some record company would reissue it. Among modern performers, Felicity Lott and Graham Johnson understand the Poulenc style, as does François Le Roux, a fine French baritone. Recordings by Bernac's student, the Dutch baritone Bernard Kruysen, on Warner-Erato also merit reprinting. The BBC might consider transferring to CD performances in its archives by Peter Pears and Benjamin Britten of Poulenc's songs. Only Georges Prêtre's recordings give a fair idea of the orchestral works, but it is hoped that the French INA will publish performances by Manuel Rosenthal and others in their archives. Wanda Landowska's version of the *Concert champêtre*, conducted by Leopold Stokowski for Decca, remains sadly out of print, like Roger Désormière's legendary *Les Biches* on Decca. Among the choral works, *Sept Répons des ténèbres* awaits a definitive recording. Poulenc accompanied Denise Duval in a delightful recital for the Mai musical de Bordeaux, 1958 which made a fugitive appearance on CD from a small French company, Clio, but is currently out of print.

Opera

Les Mamelles de Tirésias
Denise Duval (soprano), Jean Giraudeau (tenor); chorus and orchestra of the Opéra-Comique conducted by André Cluytens; with *Le Bal masqué*
EMI CDM 565565 2

Dialogues des Carmélites
Denise Duval (soprano), Régine Crespin (soprano), Denise Scharley (contralto), Liliane Berton (soprano), Rita Gorr (mezzo-soprano), Xavier Depraz (bass), Paul Finel (tenor); chorus and orchestra of the Opéra de Paris conducted by Pierre Dervaux
EMI 7493312

La Voix humaine
Denise Duval (soprano); orchestra of the Opéra-Comique conducted by Georges Prêtre; with a Jean Cocteau monologue, *Le Bel indifférent*, recited by Edith Piaf
EMI CDM 7696962

La Voix humaine
Jane Rhodes (soprano); Orchestre National de France conducted by Jean-Pierre Marty
INA Mémoire Vive 262019

Vocal Music

Le Bal masqué
Pierre Bernac (baritone); Francis Poulenc (piano), chamber musicians from the orchestra of the Opéra de Paris conducted by Louis Frémaux; with the *Elégie* for horn and piano, Sonata for flute and piano, Trio for oboe, bassoon and piano
Adès 140522

Dans le jardin d'Anna
Allons plus vite
Le Bestiaire
Le Pont
Monparnasse
La Grenouillière
Les Banalités
Epitaphe
Calligrammes
Chansons gaillardes
Priez pour paix
Pierre Bernac (baritone); Francis Poulenc (piano)
ADÈS 1411442

Cinq Poèmes
La Fraîcheur et le Feu
Tu vois le feu du soir
Tel Jour, telle nuit
Le Disparu
Paul et Virginie
Parisiana
C'est ainsi que tu es
Le Travail du peintre
Pierre Bernac (baritone); Francis Poulenc (piano)
ADÈS 141152

Le Bestiaire
Chansons gaillardes
Tel Jour, telle nuit
Pierre Bernac (baritone); Francis Poulenc (piano)
EMI 7546052

C
À Sa Guitare
Hugues Cuénod (tenor); Geoffrey Parsons (piano)
In December 1953, Cuénod recorded a Poulenc recital accompanied by the composer for Swiss Radio, who would do well to reprint this document
NIMBUS NI 5027

Le Bestiaire
Camille Maurane (baritone); György Sebök (piano)
WARNER-ERATO WPCC-3391-6

La Dame de Monte Carlo
Le Bestiaire
Cocardes, etc.
Felicity Lott (soprano); Graham Johnson (piano)
FORLANE UCD 16730

Main dominée par le coeur
Tu vois le feu du soir
Leontyne Price (soprano); David Garvey (piano)
BMG 09026 61499 2

Le Bestiaire
Claire Croiza (soprano); Francis Poulenc (piano); with *Airs chantés* Suzanne Peignot (soprano), Francis Poulenc (piano); with, among others, *Aubade, Deux novellettes,* Trio for piano, oboe and bassoon, *Trois mouvements perpétuels*
PEARL GEMM CD 9311

Choral works

Mass in G
Quatre Motets pour un temps de Noël
Quatre Motets pour un temps de Pénitence
Quatre Petites Prières de Saint François d'Assise
Robert Shaw Chorale and Orchestra conducted by Robert Shaw
TELARC CD-80236

Gloria
Litanies à la Vierge noire
Quatre Motets pour un temps de Noël, etc.
The Cambridge Singers
The City of London Sinfonia conducted by John Rutter
COLLEGIUM COLCD 108

Orchestral works

Concerto for Two Pianos
Francis Poulenc and Jacques Février (pianos), Orchestre de la Société des Concerts du Conservatoire conducted by Georges Prêtre; with *Les Biches, Les Animaux modèles* and the *Concert champêtre*
EMI CZS 7626902

Concerto for Organ
Maurice Duruflé (organ), Orchestre National de l'O.R.T.F. conducted by Georges Prêtre; with *Gloria, Quatre Motets pour un temps de Pénitence*
EMI CDC 747723 2

Piano

Trois Mouvements perpétuels
Marcelle Meyer (piano)
EMI CZS 7674052B

Trois Mouvements perpétuels
Intermezzos
Arthur Rubinstein (piano)
BMG 09026 61446 2

Presto
Vladimir Horowitz (piano)
BMG GD60377

Sonata for two pianos
Sonata for piano duet
Gabriel Tacchino and Jacques Février (piano); with other two piano works
EMI CDM 7639462

Trois Mouvements perpétuels
Nocturne No. 1
Suite française
Francis Poulenc (piano)
Sony MPK 47684

Deux Novellettes
Nocturnes
Improvisations
Francis Poulenc (piano); with Trio for piano, oboe and bassoon
EMI CDC 5550362

Chamber Music

Complete Chamber Music
Jacques Février (piano), Yehudi Menuhin (violin), Maurice Gendron (cello), Michel Portal (clarinet), Michel Debost (flute), Amaury Wallez (bassoon), Maurice Bourgue (oboe)
EMI 7627362

Sextet
Trio
Sonata for flute and piano
Sonata for oboe and piano
Sonata for clarinet and piano
Pascal Rogé (piano), Patrick Gallois (flute), Maurice Bourgue (oboe), Michel Portal (clarinet), Amaury Wallez (bassoon), André Cazalet (horn)
Decca 4215812

Miscellaneous

Histoire de Babar
Peter Ustinov (narrator); Orchestre de Paris conducted by Georges Prêtre, orchestrated by Jean Françaix
EMI CDM 7631572

Five Debussy Songs
Bernard Kruysen (baritone); Francis Poulenc (piano)
INA Mémoire Vive 262010

Trois Valses Romantiques: Chabrier
Marcelle Meyer and Francis Poulenc (pianos)
EMI CZS 7674052A

Francis Poulenc ou l'Invité de Touraine: Entretiens avec Claude Rostand
Paris, Éditions INA/Radio-France 211734 (1995)

Francis Poulenc par lui-même
speech given at the offices of Boosey and Hawkes, Paris on 10 January 1962
Paris, L'Association des Amis de Francis Poulenc, two audio-cassettes (1988)

Index

Page numbers in italic refer to picture captions.

Photographic Acknowledgements

Cecil Beaton Photographs, courtesy of Sotheby's, London: 33, 70, 103, 105, 160
The Bridgeman Art Library/ Giraudon: *Guernica* (1937) by Pablo Picasso, Museo Nacional Centro de Arte Reina Sofia, Madrid: 132–3
The Bridgeman Art Library/ Hermitage, St Petersburg: *La Danse* (1910) by Henri Matisse: 156
Jean-Loup Charmet, Paris: 109
Christie's Images, London: 85
Drawing appeared in *The Dial*: 18
Galerie Louis Carré et Cie, Paris; Jacques Villon, *Mon Portrait* (1934), drawing, 245 x 225 cm: 196
Éditions Gallimard: 150
Hulton Getty, London: 24r, 88–9, 115, 120–1
Kunstmuseum, Basel; Paul Klee, *Kühlung in einem Garten der heißen Zone* (1924), ink and watercolour, 29.6 x 20.7 cm; Marc Chagall, *The Cattle Dealer* (1912), oil on canvas, 97 x 200.5 cm: 196
The Lebrecht Collection: 65, 217
Moderna Museet, Stockholm; Joan Miró, *La Figure rouge* (1927), oil on canvas, 112 x 144 cm: 196
Museum of Modern Art, NY; Pablo Picasso, *Les Demoiselles d'Avignon* (1906–7), oil on canvas, 96 x 92 in.: 196
Musée National d'Art Moderne, Paris; Georges Braque, *Still Life with Playing Cards* (1913), oil and charcoal on canvas, 32 x 23 5/8 in.: 196
Collection Francis Poulenc, Paris: 2, 11, 13, 37, 40l+r, 59, 64, 67–8, 95, 111, 118, 139, 147, 154–5, 163, 166, 173, 208, 211, 214–5, 220–1/Denis Manceaux 193
Private Collection, London: 20, 20–1, 35, 51–3, 72–3
©Estate of Man Ray: 78
Collection Yves Saint Laurent/Pierre Bergé: 159
Roger-Viollet, Paris: 29, 31, 46, 81, 123, 128, 131, 136
Photograph by René-Jean Ségalat, Paris: 143
Photographs by Leslie E. Spatt: 205, 206–7
Staatsgalerie Stuttgart; Juan Gris, *The Eggs* (1912), oil on canvas, 22.5 x 15 in.: 196
Studio Vista: 98
Photographs by Theatre Museum, V&A, London: 54, 55, 169, 176–7, 180, 181, 182, 184–5, 187, 190–1
From *L'Histoire de Babar, le petit éléphant* by Jean de Brunhoff © Librairie Hachette, 1939: 141, 144–5, 222